Web-Based Learning
in K-12 Classrooms:
Opportunities and Challenges

Web-Based Learning in K-12 Classrooms: Opportunities and Challenges has been co-published simultaneously as *Computers in the Schools*, Volume 21, Numbers 3/4 2004.

Web-Based Learning in K-12 Classrooms: Opportunities and Challenges

Jay Blanchard, PhD
James Marshall, PhD
Editors

Web-Based Learning in K-12 Classrooms: Opportunities and Challenges has been co-published simultaneously as *Computers in the Schools*, Volume 21, Numbers 3/4 2004.

Routledge
Taylor & Francis Group
New York   London

First published by

The Haworth Press, Inc., 10 Alice Street, Binghamton, NY 13904-1580

This edition published 2012 by Routledge

Routledge
Taylor & Francis Group
711 Third Avenue
New York, NY 10017

Routledge
Taylor & Francis Group
2 Park Square, Milton Park
Abingdon, Oxon OX14 4RN

Web-Based Learning in K-12 Classrooms: Opportunities and Challenges has been co-published simultaneously as *Computers in the Schools*, Volume 21, Numbers 3/4 2004.

The development, preparation, and publication of this work has been undertaken with great care. However, the publisher, employees, editors, and agents of The Haworth Press and all imprints of The Haworth Press, Inc., including The Haworth Medical Press® and Pharmaceutical Products Press®, are not responsible for any errors contained herein or for consequences that may ensue from use of materials or information contained in this work. Opinions expressed by the author(s) are not necessarily those of The Haworth Press, Inc. With regard to case studies, identities and circumstances of individuals discussed herein have been changed to protect confidentiality. Any resemblance to actual persons, living or dead, is entirely coincidental.

Cover design by Kerry E. Mack

Library of Congress Cataloging-in-Publication Data

Web-based learning in K-12 classrooms : opportunities and challenges / Jay Blanchard, James Marshall, editors.
    p. cm.
    "Co-published simultaneously as Computers in the schools, volume 21, numbers 3/4 2004."
    Includes bibliographical references and index.
    ISBN 0-7890-2492-6 (hard cover : alk. paper)–ISBN 0-7890-2493-4 (soft cover : alk. paper)
  1. Education–Computer network resources. 2. Internet in education. 3. Web-based instruction.
I. Blanchard, Jay S. II. Marshall, James, 1965- III. Computers in the schools.

LB1044.87.W353 2005
371.33′4–dc22

2005003399

Web-Based Learning
in K-12 Classrooms:
Opportunities and Challenges

Contents

ABOUT THE EDITORS

Jay Blanchard, PhD, is Professor in the Psychology in Education Division, College of Education at Arizona State University in Tempe, Arizona. His PhD is in reading education from the University of Georgia. Dr. Blanchard has written numerous books, chapters and articles on technology applications in education, especially those that relate to reading education. In the 1970s he coauthored one of the first books on technology applications in reading and has continued to write about technology issues through the decades. He has been a consultant for many companies involved in educational technology including IBM, Microsoft, Plato, Pearson, and Texas Instruments–and a host of technology companies that no longer exist. He was the first chair of the International Reading Association's Technology Committee. He is a principal investigator on two U.S. Department of Education Early Reading First grants (Gadsden, Arizona; Navajo Nation, Window Rock, Arizona) and both grants are using DVD-based technologies to feature staff development.

James Marshall, PhD, is an Adjunct Faculty Member in the Department of Educational Technology at San Diego State University and an independent consultant to corporate business entities and school systems. He teaches graduate-level courses in instructional design, program evaluation, teaching with technology and organizational performance. He also serves as lead evaluator for three U.S. Department of Education grants that cover diverse topics–from technology literacy to teaching American history. Dr. Marshall's 2002 white paper, commissioned by Cable in the Classroom, entitled *Learning with Technology: Evidence that Technology Can, and Does, Support Learning*, explored the antecedents of the instructional technologies we know today. It offered historical and contemporary evidence of impact in an effort to inform educators, cable executives, and legislators alike. The paper was distributed to each member of congress and, by formal request, to Federal Communications Commissioners and executive members of the National Association of Elementary School Principals.

INTRODUCTION

Jay Blanchard

The beginning of the Internet age was hailed as a marvelous opportunity for all students and teachers to improve learning and teaching. Advocates for Web-based learning and teaching have insisted that it will transform every aspect of classroom life by "creat[ing] rich and compelling learning opportunities that meet all learners' needs and provide knowledge and training when and where it is needed, while boosting the productivity of learning and lowering its cost" (U.S. Department of Commerce, 2002, p. 11). Unfortunately, these advocates have underestimated the challenges and overestimated the opportunities and costs for schools (Oppenheimer, 2003). This *estimation error* is also true of Web-based learning in the world of business and commerce (see www. e-learningcentre.co.uk for links to discussions).

Undoubtedly, the Web is a powerful, complex set of digit technologies that has the potential to improve teaching and learning–but realizing the potential has not occurred.

Today almost every K-12 public school in the United States and many in the industrialized world have broadband Web access (Bennett, 2003; Grunwald Associates, 2003; NetDay, 2003; Pew, 2004; U.S. National Cen-

---

JAY BLANCHARD is Professor, Division of Psychology in Education, College of Education, Arizona State University, Tempe, AZ 85287-0611 (E-mail: jsb46@asu.edu).

[Haworth co-indexing entry note]: "Introduction." Blanchard, Jay. Co-published simultaneously in *Computers in the Schools* (The Haworth Press, Inc.) Vol. 21, No. 3/4, 2004, pp. 1-4; and: *Web-Based Learning in K-12 Classrooms: Opportunities and Challenges* (ed: Jay Blanchard, and James Marshall) The Haworth Press, Inc., 2004, pp. 1-4. Single or multiple copies of this article are available for a fee from The Haworth Document Delivery Service [1-800-HAWORTH, 9:00 a.m. - 5:00 p.m. (EST). E-mail address: docdelivery@haworthpress.com].

Digital Object Identifier: 10.1300/J025v21n03_01

ter for Education Statistics, 2003). But access does not guarantee acquisition of knowledge. While Web-based learning has the potential to offer meaningful, long-term solutions for schools, it continues to be a tall task. Yet discussions, research, and attempts to chronicle Web-based resources have begun. For example, the California Learning Resources Network offers an overview of some resources (www. clrn.org) as does the Schools of California Online Resources for Education (SCORE; www.score.k12.ca.us).

In the case of K-12 schools, we know that the wide range of Web-based learning opportunities (formal courses, demonstrations, simulations, collaboration, searches, etc.) has been very expensive, very slow to develop, and very time consuming to implement (Norris, Sullivan, Poirot, & Soloway, 2003). We also know that Web-based learning will not replace the caring and engaging teacher who offers instructionally effective opportunities for learning–or family members that care deeply about helping. It will not replace the human interactions inherent in classrooms. Placing a student in front of a computer or monitor is not a substitute for the world of classroom learning but instead is simply one part of it. Nevertheless, the journey from mainframes and personal computers to broadband and the Internet has begun–and so has the pressure on schools to adopt technology solutions that will cure the educational ills of the world's children. Tall task for technology!

This volume chronicles the opportunities and challenges that have emerged in Web-based learning and should offer insight for up-and-coming discussions about its future. Papers focus on K-12 content areas, namely, reading, science, mathematics, and social studies. In addition, they discuss special education, counseling, virtual schools, exemplary schools, implementation issues in schools, and guidance for schools about educational Web sites. In a final note, this volume was completed in August 2004 and care was taken to check all content for accuracy up to that date.

FUTURE CHALLENGES

High-speed, broadband capacity is present in some schools and growing in others. But, the needs are present and growing too. Will Web-based learning rise to the challenges faced by today's K-12 educators? Or, will it continue to loom on the periphery of classrooms around the world? Some supporters say *yes*, technology will revolutionize the way schools do the business of teaching. Others say *no or* couch their critiques in a cautionary view (Oppenheimer, 2003). This volume has chronicled the emergence of Web-based learning in K-12 schools and classrooms. Despite attempts by the authors, many questions remain. Here are a few.

Technology

In many countries of the world the technological infrastructure is ready, or nearly ready, to support broadband content (Bennett, 2003; Grunwald Associates, 2003; NetDay, 2003; Pew, 2004; U.S. National Center for Education Statistics, 2003). Yet, will this technology infrastructure support worldwide learning while at the same time growing and making technological advances during growth? A very difficult task!

Content

Searches for Web-based learning content and curricula outlined herein suggest a largely fragmented body of resources. With infrastructure in place, will available content increase? Will content developers choose to recycle and repurpose existing materials? Or, will they work to exploit benefits and features unique to Web-based learning? With access anywhere, anytime, the hope is the latter.

Implementation

Complementary to effective content is purposeful use. How will schools ensure programs are used–and used effectively? Blurring of the physical classroom's boundaries and extension of the learning day into the home all pose implementation challenges that must be met.

The future will continue to dictate the challenges faced by Web-based learning as it becomes more commonplace in our K-12 world. At present, the Web is used by our young people primarily at home and primarily for games, communication, and information searches. Will the chatting and browsing expand to include more school-based learning activities? While many questions remain unanswered, the potential of the Web for addressing education's needs and challenges clearly exceeds the sum of the challenges that lie ahead.

REFERENCES

Bennett, M. (2003). *A broadband world*. Washington, DC: Alliance for Public Technology. (with Benton Foundation)

Grunwald Associates. (2003). Connected to the future: A report on children's Internet use. Retrieved April 16, 2004, from the Corporation for Public Broadcasting, http://cpb.org/ed/resources/connected.

NetDay. (2003). Voices & views from today's tech-savvy students. Retrieved April 10, 2004, from www.netday.org.

Norris, C., Sullivan, T., Poirot, J., & Soloway, E. (2003). No access, no use, no impact: Snapshot surveys of educational technology in K12. *Journal of Research on Technology in Education, 36*(1), 21-30.

Oppenheimer, T. (2003). *The flickering mind*. New York: Random House.

Pew. (2001). *The Internet and education*. Washington, DC: Pew Charitable Trusts.

Pew. (2002). *The digital disconnect: The widening gap between Internet-savvy students and their schools*. Washington, DC: Pew Charitable Trusts.

Pew. (2003). *America's online pursuits*. Washington, DC: Pew Charitable Trusts.

Pew. (2004). *Internet & American life* (Internet Tracking Data, April 13, 2004). Washington, DC: Pew Charitable Trusts.

U.S. Department of Commerce. (2002, September 23). *Office of Technology Policy Report*. Washington, DC: Author.

U.S. National Center for Education Statistics (NCES). (2003). *Internet access in public schools and classrooms: 1994-2002*. Washington, DC: Author.

Jay Blanchard
Jared McLain
Patrick Bartshe

The Web and Reading Instruction

SUMMARY. This paper briefly chronicles the marriage of technology and reading instruction and then turns to focus on Web-based reading instruction. Issues are discussed that relate to reading effectiveness research, the U.S. No Child Left Behind legislation, the U.S. National Educational Technology Effectiveness Study, and the state of Web-based reading instruction, including the lack of a research base. *[Article copies available for a fee from The Haworth Document Delivery Service: 1-800-HAWORTH. E-mail address: <docdelivery@haworthpress.com> Website: <http://www.HaworthPress.com> © 2004 by The Haworth Press, Inc. All rights reserved.]*

KEYWORDS. Web, K-8 reading instruction, Internet, broadband

JAY BLANCHARD is Professor, Division of Psychology in Education, College of Education, Arizona State University, Tempe, AZ 85287-0611 (E-mail: jsb46@asu.edu).
JARED MCLAIN is a doctoral student, Division of Psychology in Education, College of Education, Arizona State University, Tempe, AZ 85287-0611 (E-mail: jared.mclain@asu.edu).
PATRICK BARTSHE is a doctoral student, Division of Psychology in Education, College of Education, Arizona State University, Tempe, AZ 85287-0611 (E-mail: Patrick.Bartshe@asu.edu).

[Haworth co-indexing entry note]: "The Web and Reading Instruction." Blanchard, Jay, Jared McLain, and Patrick Bartshe. Co-published simultaneously in *Computers in the Schools* (The Haworth Press, Inc.) Vol. 21, No. 3/4, 2004, pp. 5-14; and: *Web-Based Learning in K-12 Classrooms: Opportunities and Challenges* (ed: Jay Blanchard, and James Marshall) The Haworth Press, Inc., 2004, pp. 5-14. Single or multiple copies of this article are available for a fee from The Haworth Document Delivery Service [1-800-HAWORTH, 9:00 a.m. - 5:00 p.m. (EST). E-mail address: docdelivery@haworthpress.com].

http://www.haworthpress.com/web/CITS
© 2004 by The Haworth Press, Inc. All rights reserved.
Digital Object Identifier: 10.1300/J025v21n03_02

The marriage of technology and K-12 reading instruction has a long and storied history (Blanchard, 1999; Blanchard & Daniel, 1982; Blanchard & Mason, 1987; Johnson, 2003; Labbo, 2000; Maddux, 2003; Mason, 1987; Mason & Blanchard, 1979; Willis, 2003). In the last century, it began with the telephone, phonograph, and radio and moved to film, talking typewriters, and on to TV. It continued with the electronic and digital applications of the mainframe computer, the desktop and laptop computer, and finally wireless PDA computers (Blanchard, 1999; Cuban, 1986; Oppenheimer, 2003). Today the marriage includes broadband, high-capacity, always-on, two-way, Internet-based technologies (provided by cable modem, telephone line, satellite, fixed and terrestrial wireless, fiber optics) and applications that have come to be called Web-based e-learning (Grunwald Associates, 2003). Simply put, this means the computer is a connectivity platform or, perhaps, a gateway that allows students, teachers, or anyone to originate and receive high-quality, voice, data, graphics, and video telecommunications for reading through the Web. Web-based applications join earlier delivery systems like CDs, servers, and peripheral devices (e.g., LeapFrog). Unfortunately, the technologies of these earlier delivery systems have not guaranteed reading success for all students. This lack of a guarantee has not gone unnoticed by the U.S. Department of Education, Institute of Education Sciences (IES), which has just launched a three-year, 10 million dollar independent study of educational technology effectiveness, including the study of several programs with Web-based reading instruction (contractor, www.mathmatica-mpr.com). In an overstatement of the obvious, the Benton Foundation and the Alliance for Public Technology, in *Broadband World* (Bennett, 2003), reached the conclusion that "simply having an internet connection in a classroom does not automatically translate to an enhanced educational environment" (p. 11).

A BRIEF HISTORY

The first application of computer technology to K-12 reading instruction occurred in the 1960s and 1970s with University of Illinois (Illiac-1) and Stanford University (PDP-1) efforts to add beginning reading and mathematics learning. Along the way, Control Data Corporation, IBM, Digital Equipment Corporation, Sperry-Univac, RCA, GE, and HP all got into the act in some degree or the other (Mason, Blanchard & Daniel, 1982). Two reading systems that sprang from these initial efforts were today's PLATO and Pearson Digital Learning (formerly, Computer Curriculum Corporation). All these early efforts were much heralded across the

United States and, indeed, the world. All were mainframe, time-sharing technologies featuring Skinnerian-type drill-and-practice applications. From those halcyon days forward, technology has been a part of reading. Rightly or wrongly, all these early technologies and applications have contributed to Web-based efforts (Cuban, 1986, 2001). Thus, the notion that reading instruction could be delivered from sources outside the classroom by technology is not new. What is new is the ability to deliver quality teaching and learning via the Web.

The appearance of Web-based e-learning has spelled changes for K-12 reading instruction. Schools and households, in particular, have gained more choice. School-based technologies and applications from the 1970s, 1980s, and 1990s have slowly given way to anytime, anywhere, two-way learning. Older applications, like server-based, integrated learning system (ILS; see Estep, McInerney, Vockell, & Kosmoski, 1999) or external storage devices like CDs are still available, but will become less and less common as more applications are transferred to Web-based technologies.

The North Central Regional Educational Laboratory (NCREL) has chronicled many of the changes in computer-based reading. NCREL believes three phases are at work today (NCREL, 2000). Phase one (print automation) features drill-and-practice applications with technology as the teacher and students as passive learners. Phase two (expansion of learning opportunities) features learner-centered, tool-based activities rather than the passive delivery of content. Technology is a tool in the hands of students and teachers. Phase three is data-driven virtual learning. This phase is marked by the use of the Internet for learning and teaching as well as management of information. NCREL suggested that this phase "is in an early stage of very rapid development and is now accumulating quality research" (p. 1, Phase III). The U.S. Department of Education has also chronicled educational technology in *A Retrospective on Twenty Years of Education Technology Policy* (Culp, Honey, & Mandinach, 2003). The report concluded that two themes emerged about educational technology. With editorial license, these themes can be combined into one: K-12 education needs are always changing and these needs must drive technology solutions. Or, perhaps simply put, technology must solve more problems than it creates.

EFFECTIVENESS

Attempts to answer questions about which problems are solved by technology, which problems are created, fall under the category of effectiveness studies. Historically, these studies have reached three general conclusions. First and foremost is the conclusion that the marriage of reading and technologies works well (Blok, Oostdam, Otter, & Overmatt, 2002; see also Kulik, 1994; Roblyer, Castine, & King, 1988; Ryan, 1991; Sivin-Kachela & Bialo, 1996; Waxman, Connell, & Gray, 2002; Waxman, Lin, & Michko, 2003). A second conclusion indicates that it does not (Cordes & Miller, 2000; Cuban, 2001; Oppenheimer, 2003; Paterson, Henry, O'Quin, Ceprano, & Blue, 2003; Schmitt & Slonaker, 1996). A third conclusion is cautionary: Technology can help but it depends upon a number of variables that are difficult to control (Keltner & Ross, 1996; Norris, Sullivan, Poirot, & Soloway, 2003; Pflaum, 2004; Waxman, Lin, & Michko, 2003; Zhao & Frank, 2003). For example, Lou, Abrami, and Apoonia (2001) completed a meta-analysis of small group learning versus individual learning in technology-based settings. The researchers found that small group settings were more effective than individual ones for learning with technology. (This meta-analysis included a number of reading instruction studies from pre-K to high school.)

What is missing, of course, are a significant number of scientifically based investigations of Web-based K-12 reading instruction. The reason is simple: The broadband, high-capacity, always-on, two-way technologies and subsequent applications are too new. The most recent meta-analysis of educational technology effectiveness data (re: Waxman, Lin, & Michko, 2003) does not address the question. Furthermore, most recent commentary is silent on the issue (Leu, Kinzer, Coiro, & Cammack, 2004). Searches of academic databases in April 2004 revealed no specific research on Web-based reading instruction in K-12. This suggests that much needs to be done, but a few answers should soon emerge.

The U.S. Department of Education, Institute of Education Sciences (2003) has launched a multi-year, multi-million dollar study of educational technology effectiveness. The U.S. No Child Left Behind law requires that funds used by schools to purchase educational programs and products must demonstrate effectiveness: Hence, the purpose of the study. Two focuses of the study are early reading-Grade 1 (six-year-olds) and reading comprehension-Grade 4 (nine-year-olds). At present, the early reading products under scrutiny are: (a) Academy of Reading (AutoSkill), (b) Destination Reading (Riverdeep), (c) Waterford Early Reading (Waterford), (d) Headsprout Early Reading (Headsprout), and (e) Plato FOCUS (Plato Learning). Two of the five have Web-based instruction programs (i.e., Destination Reading, Headsprout). The comprehension programs are

(a) Academy of Reading (AutoSkill), (b) Read 180 (Scholastic), (c) KnowledgeBox (Pearson), and (d) Leaptrack (LeapFrog). Unfortunately, only one offers Web-based instruction (Pearson). Nevertheless, this study should help answer questions about Web-based reading, including which attributes it shares, or does not share, with its technology cousins that do not use the Web (for example, see reviews by Ross, Hogaboam-Gray, & Hanny, 2001, of Scholastic's WiggleWorks; and Paterson et al., 2003, of Pearson Digital Learning's Waterford Early Reading).

The Institute of Education Sciences study is a result of the *No Child Left Behind Act of 2001*. NCLB mandates that programs be evaluated using scientifically based research principles, and only those programs judged effective through these principles can be used. The term *scientifically based research* appears a total of 111 times in the NCLB legislation. Attempts to explain what all this means have appeared in the Institute of Education Sciences' *Identifying and Implementing Educational Practices Supported by Rigorous Evidence: A User Friendly Guide* (2003; see also National Research Council, 2002). According to the *Guide*, scientifically based research involves the application of rigorous, systematic, and objective procedures that bring about reliable, valid, and replicable knowledge. Research principles that must be applied to judge Web-based reading programs include: (a) systematic, empirical methods that draw on observation or experiment; (b) rigorous, independent analyses that are adequate to test stated hypotheses and justify conclusions drawn; (c) measurements or observational methods that provide reliable and valid data across evaluators and observers, and across multiple measurements and studies; (d) experimental or quasi-experimental designs in which individuals, entities, programs, or activities are assigned to different conditions and with appropriate controls to evaluate the effects of the condition of interest, with a preference for random assignment experiments; (e) experimental studies with sufficient detail and clarity to allow for replication; and (f) rigorous, objective scientific reviews in peer-reviewed journals or approval by a panel of independent experts. Quite a list of principles for programs and products! However, it should be noted that the NCLB Law section on technology (Title II, Section D) is silent on principles or guidelines for Web-based reading instruction beyond those generally stated for all programs and products.

A BEGINNING

Today's Web-generation teachers and students are comfortable with Internet access and the freedoms it brings. In fact, they reject passive participation and expect active control over applications, whether e-mails, information searches, or games (Healy, 1998; Tapscott, 1998).

In U.S. homes and businesses, survey data indicate 65% of U.S. adults use the Web (Pew, 2004). This helps explain why over 75% of students between the ages of 12 and 17 use the Web (see also, Bennett, 2003; Grunwald Associates, 2003; Oblinger, 2003; Pew, 2003). Supporting the Pew data, the NetDay (2003) survey of 210,000 students from 3,000 schools (October-November 2003) found that students use the Internet at home, primarily for communication, games, and information searches. If these data are correct, school use of the Web needs to improve.

Regardless of where the Web is used, some questions need answers. Most notably for this discussion: How is the Web used for reading instruction? This question also interests the editors of *Technology and Learning* magazine. The magazine has begun to report on Web-based "literacy" activities. For example, in the September 15, 2002, issue, Lafferty discussed reading instruction activities (Plato-Lightspan, Compass Learning). In the June 16, 2003, issue, more activities were reviewed (Compass Learning, Plato-Lightspan, istation, Pearson, Riverdeep, Scholastic). A more recent issue of *Technology and Learning* (January 15, 2004) discussed Compass Learning, Headsprout, istation, and Riverdeep reading activities. Another magazine, *Multimedia Schools*, simply changed names (January 2004) to reflect a new focus on Web-based e-learning in the schools. It is now called *Multimedia & Internet@Schools*. In addition, *60 Great Internet Sites for Math, Reading, and Language Arts* (Treadwell, 2002) may be the first book to review and evaluate K-12 reading instruction Web sites.

Education journals of teacher organizations and associations are beginning to chronicle Web-based reading instruction too! Perhaps the first article on Web-based reading instruction appeared in a themed issue of the International Reading Association's (IRA) journal, *Reading Teacher*, entitled "Owning Technology" (April 2002). In the issue, Dufflemeyer (2002) discusses Web-based emergent reading and alphabet skills. According to Dufflemeyer, the Web is rife with opportunities to help children learn to read. Focusing his article on using the Web to teach letters and sounds, Dufflemeyer discusses the importance of letters and sounds in learning to read and describes ten Web sites that can help (ABC Order, Alphabet Chart, Animated ABCs, Haunted Alphabet, There Are the Letters of the Alphabet, Morris Farm Alphabet, Alphabet Action, Hidden Letters, Alphabet Soup, and Alphabet Presentation). He notes that the sites feature the standard fare of motivational content and many have audio support. Adding to the strength of the discussion, Dufflemeyer offers suggestions on how teachers might use the sites for blended instruction, thereby integrating the Web-based content with traditional classroom content (see Leander, 2003, and Ryan, Kloss, Chorost, & Fried, 2002, for a discussion of blended). In the same issue, McVee and Dickson (2002) offer a rubric for examining literacy software for primary grades that could be adapted for use with Web-based reading instruction. Recently, IRA published *Cartwheels on the Keyboard: Computer-Based Literacy Instruction in an Elementary Classroom* (Carroll, 2004). The book describes one classroom teacher's efforts using technology for literacy development with examples of Web-based applications.

IRA also sponsors a Web-based journal entitled *Reading Online* (www.readingonline.org) and has published a *Position Statement on Integrating Literacy and Technology in the Curriculum* that provides some direction for Web-based reading (see www.reading.org). However, while *Reading Online* features articles and discussions about technology and reading, it has not yet tackled Web-based reading instruction. Nor have articles in IRA's chief research journal, *Reading Research Quarterly* (RRQ). While one issue of RRQ focused on Web-based literacy, no mention was made of Web-based reading instruction (Vol. 38, No. 3, 2002). In the near future, hopefully, more *Reading Online* articles and more articles like Dufflemeyer's will appear. Another hope is that academic and research-based journals, as well as organizations interested in technology education for teachers, such as the International Society for Technology in Education (ISTE) and the Society for Information Technology and Teacher Education (SITE), will begin to investigate and critically evaluate Web-based reading instruction.

CONCLUSION

Web-based K-12 reading instruction is a potential beacon of innovation in a chaotic world of challenges, and, obviously, teachers and students are starting to use it. For examples, www.AOL@school.com, www.Scholastic.com (kidsfunonline), and www.rif.org/readingplanet now offer reading activities on their Web sites. The George Lucas Education Foundation has begun to chronicle innovative examples of reading applications (www.GLEF.org) in *edutopia* and *edutopia online*; Intel, in the *Innovator*; and Microsoft, in the *Educator Newsletter*.

These examples are a very small number of potential classrooms and schools. Where are the rest? The U.S. National Research Council's Steering Committee on Improving Learning and Information Technology Report (2002) suggests that "when teachers find a new product or educational strategy that makes a difference, they will adopt it instantly" (p. 18). Clearly, what this means is, build a good Web-based reading instruction program and teachers will use it. They do not have to be ordered to use it, cajoled to use it, or paid to use it. They will use it because it helps them teach reading and helps their students become better readers. There is no greater challenge in education than to ensure that all children across the globe have the best possible opportunity to learn to read and to continue to improve as readers. If the broadband, Web era fulfills only one of its innovative promises–that would be the best one!

REFERENCES

Bennett, M. (2003). *A broadband world*. Washington, DC: Alliance for Public Technology. (with Benton Foundation)

Blanchard, J. (Ed.). (1999). *Educational computing in the schools: Technology, communication and literacy*. New York: Haworth Press.

Blanchard, J., & Mason, G. (Eds.). (1987). *The computer in reading and language arts*. New York: Haworth Press.

Blok, H., Oostdam, R., Otter, M., & Overmatt, M. (2002). Computer-assisted instruction in support of beginning reading instruction: A review. *Review of Educational Research, 72*, 101-130.

Carroll, M. (2004). *Cartwheels on the keyboard: Computer-based literacy instruction in an elementary classroom*. Newark, DE: International Reading Association.

Cordes, C., & Miller, E. (2000). *Fool's gold: A critical look at computers in childhood*. College Park, MD: Alliance for Childhood.

Cuban, L. (1986). *Teachers and machines: The classroom use of technology since 1920*. New York: Teachers College Press.

Cuban, L. (2001). *Oversold and underused: Computers in the classroom*. Cambridge, MA: Harvard Press.

Culp, K., Honey, M., & Mandinach, E. (2003). *A retrospective on twenty years of educational technology policy*. Washington, DC: U.S. Department of Education, Office of Educational Technology.

Dufflemeyer, F. (2002). Alphabet activities on the Internet. *Reading Teacher, 55*(7), 631-635.

Estep, S., McInerney, W., Vockell, E., & Kosmoski, G. (1999). An investigation of the relationship between integrated learning systems and academic achievement. *Journal of Educational Technology Systems, 28*(1), 5-19.

Grunwald Associates. (2003). *Connected to the future: A report on children's Internet use*. Retrieved April 16, 2004, from the Corporation for Public Broadcasting http://cpb.org/ed/resources/connected.

Healy, J. (1998). *Failure to connect: How computers affect our children's minds for better or worse.* New York: Simon & Schuster.

Johnson, L. (2003). The dream machine. *Computers in the Schools, 20*(1/2), 1-10.

Keltner, B., & Ross, R. (1996). *The cost of school-based educational technology programs.* Santa Monica, CA: RAND.

Kulik, J. (1994). Meta-analytic studies of findings on computer-based instruction. In E. Baker & H. O'Neil (Eds.), *Technology assessment in education and training* (pp. 9-33). Hillsdale, NJ: Erlbaum.

Labbo, L. (2000). *Toward a vision of the future role of technology in literacy education. Forum on Technology in Education.* Washington, DC: U.S. Department of Education, Office of Educational Technology.

Leander, K. (2003). Writing travelers' tales on new literacyscapes. *Reading Research Quarterly, 38*(3), 392-397.

Leu, D., Kinzer, C., Coiro, J., & Cammack, D. (2004). Toward a theory of new literacies emerging from the Internet and other information and communication technologies. In R. Ruddell & N. Unrau (Eds.), *Theoretical models and processes of reading* (pp. 1570-1613). Newark, DE: International Reading Association.

Lou, Y., Abrami, P., & Aploonia, S. (2001). Small group and individual learning with technology: A meta-analysis. *Review of Educational Research, 71*(3), 449-521.

Maddux, C. (2003). Twenty years of research in information technology in education: Assessing our progress. *Computers in the Schools, 20*(1/2), 35-48.

Mason, G., & Blanchard, J. (1979). *Computer applications in reading.* Newark, DE: International Reading Association.

Mason, G., Blanchard, J., & Daniel, D. (1982). *Computer applications in reading* (2nd ed.). Newark, DE: International Reading Association.

Mason, G., Blanchard, J., & Daniel, D. (1987). *Computer applications in reading* (3rd ed.). Newark, DE: International Reading Association.

McVee, M., & Dickson, B. (2002). Creating a rubric to examine literacy software for the primary grades. *Reading Teacher, 55*(7), 635-639.

National Research Council. (2002). *Improving learning with technology.* Washington, DC: National Academy Press.

NetDay. (2003). *Voices & views from today's tech-savvy students.* Retrieved April 10, 2004, from www.netday.org.

Norris, C., Sullivan, T., Poirot, J., & Soloway, E. (2003). No access, no use, no impact: Snapshot surveys of educational technology in K-12. *Journal of Research on Technology in Education, 36*(1), 21-30.

North Central Regional Educational Laboratory. (2000). *Computer-based technology and learning: Evolving uses and expectations.* Naperville, IL: Author.

Oblinger, D. (2003, July/August). *Boomers, Gen-Xers, and Millennials: Understanding the new students.* EDUCAUSE, 37-47.

Oppenheimer, T. (2003). *The flickering mind.* New York: Random House.

Paterson, W., Henry, J., O'Quin, K., Ceprano, M., & Blue, E. (2003). Investigating the effectiveness of an integrated learning system on early emergent readers. *Reading Research Quarterly, 38*(2), 172-207.

Pew. (2001). *The Internet and education.* Washington, DC: Pew Charitable Trusts.

Pew. (2002). *The digital disconnect: The widening gap between Internet-savvy students and their schools.* Washington, DC: Pew Charitable Trusts.

Pew. (2003). *America's online pursuits*. Washington, DC: Pew Charitable Trusts.

Pew. (2004). *Internet and American Life* (Internet Tracking Data, April 13, 2004). Washington, DC: Pew Charitable Trusts.

Pflaum, W. (2004). *The technology fix: The promise and reality of computers in our schools*. Alexandria, VA: Association for Supervision and Curriculum Development.

Roblyer, M., Castine, W., & King, F. (1988). Assessing the impact of computer-based instruction: A review of recent research. *Computers in the Schools, 5*(3-4), 117-149.

Ross, J., Hogaboam-Gray, A., & Hanny, L. (2001). Collateral benefits of an interactive literacy program for grade 1 and 2 students. *Journal of Research on Computing in Education, 33*(3), 219-234.

Ryan, A. (1991). Meta-analysis of achievement effects of micro-computer applications in elementary schools. *Educational Administration Quarterly, 27*(2), 161-184.

Ryan, P., Kloss, J., Chorost, M., & Fried, R. (2002). *Developing powerful learning solutions*. Menlo Park, CA: SRI International.

Schmitt, C., & Slonaker, L. (1996, January 14). Computers in school: Do students improve? High technology doesn't always equal high achievement. *San Jose Mercury News*, 1A.

Sivin-Kachela, J., & Bialo, E. (1996). *Report on the effectiveness of technology in the schools*. Washington, DC: Software Publishers Association.

Tapscott, D. (1998). *Growing up digital: The rise of the Net generation*. New York: McGraw-Hill.

Treadwell, M. (2002). *60 Great Internet sites for math, reading, and language arts*. Arlington Heights, IL: Skylight Professional Development.

U.S. Department of Commerce. (2002, September 23). *Office of Technology policy report*. Washington, DC: Author.

U.S. Department of Education. (2003). *A retrospective on twenty years of education technology policy*. Washington, DC: Office of Educational Technology.

U.S. Department of Education, Institute for Education Sciences. (2003). *Identifying and implementing educational practices supported by rigorous evidence: A user friendly guide*. Washington, DC: Author.

U.S. National Center for Education Statistics (NCES). (2003). *Internet access in public schools and classrooms: 1994-2002*. Washington, DC: Author.

Waxman, H., Connell, M., & Gray, J. (2002). *A quantitative synthesis of recent research on the effects of teaching and learning with technology on student outcomes*. Naperville, IL: North Central Regional Educational Laboratory.

Waxman, H., Lin, M., & Michko, G. (2003). *A meta-analysis of the effectiveness of teaching and learning with technology on student outcomes*. Naperville, IL: Learning Point Associates.

Web-Based Education Commission. (2000). *The power of the Internet for learning; Moving from promise to practice*. Washington, DC: U.S. Congress. (Legislative authority expired 3/19/2001)

Willis, J. (2003). Instructional technologies in schools: Are we there yet? *Computers in the Schools, 20*(1/2), 11-34.

Zhao, Y., & Frank, K. (2003). Factors affecting technology uses in schools: An ecological perspective. *American Educational Research Journal, 40*(4), 807-840.

Marguerite Hillman
Terry J. Moore

The Web and Early Literacy

SUMMARY. The Web as an appropriate vehicle for educating young children in formal and informal school settings is the subject of widespread, international debate (Anderson, 2000; Attewell, Suazo-Garcia, & Battle, 2003; Davis & Shade, 1994; Dolowy, 2000; Filipenko & Rolfsen, 1999; Pendleton, 2001; Vail, 2001; Wardle, 1999). Regardless of these debates, however, the Web's use in early education continues to grow. This article describes current Web usage in early education, particularly literacy education, and suggests possibilities for the future. *[Article copies available for a fee from The Haworth Document Delivery Service: 1-800-HAWORTH. E-mail address: <docdelivery@haworthpress.com> Website: <http://www.HaworthPress.com> © 2004 by The Haworth Press, Inc. All rights reserved.]*

KEYWORDS. Web and early literacy, early literacy, literacy, literacy and young children, education and the Web, technology and learning, the Internet and young children, early literacy software

---

MARGUERITE HILLMAN is CEO/President, Cosmos Literacy, Solana Beach, CA 92075 (E-mail: mhillman@cosmosliteracy.com).
TERRY J. MOORE is a doctoral student, English Department, Arizona State University, Tempe, AZ 85287 (E-mail: limerick@asu.edu).

[Haworth co-indexing entry note]: "The Web and Early Literacy." Hillman, Marguerite, and Terry J. Moore. Co-published simultaneously in *Computers in the Schools* (The Haworth Press, Inc.) Vol. 21, No. 3/4, 2004, pp. 15-21; and: *Web-Based Learning in K-12 Classrooms: Opportunities and Challenges* (ed: Jay Blanchard, and James Marshall) The Haworth Press, Inc., 2004, pp. 15-21. Single or multiple copies of this article are available for a fee from The Haworth Document Delivery Service [1-800-HAWORTH, 9:00 a.m. - 5:00 p.m. (EST). E-mail address: docdelivery@haworthpress.com].

Digital Object Identifier: 10.1300/J025v21n03_03

The wildfire spread of Web use for adults as a vehicle for communication, news, commerce, and data search and retrieval has occurred in a miniscule window of time, compared to past paradigm shifts. For instance, by the beginning of the 21st century, U.S. census data indicated that the percentage of households with computers increased from 36% to 51%. Even more remarkably, households with Web access rose from 18% to 41.5%–Web use more than doubled in three years. Census figures also show that 66% of households with school-age children had computers, and 51% of these had Web access at the turn of the century (U.S. Census Bureau, 2001). The worldwide love affair with the Web, computers, and other high-tech gadgets shows no sign of cooling off, nor is it limited to adults.

Web use by children is also widespread and increasing rapidly. For example, by September 2003, 27 million American children between the ages of 2 and 17 accessed the Web at home; 12 million were between the ages of 2 and 11 (Nielsen/NetRatings, 2003). What are the youngest of these children doing on the Web? At least 29% of K-3 students surveyed in NetDay's Speak Up Day 2003 had their own e-mail accounts (Poftack, 2004). Add Web use in preschools and early elementary school programs to the mix, both for children and their teachers, and the Web can viewed as an emerging force in early literacy.

LEARNING WITH THE WEB

Research suggests that using technology like the Web to increase literacy skills does work if used appropriately. In *Computers and Young Children*, for example, Haugland (2000a) stressed that three- and four-year-old children should use the computer to experiment, explore, and discover the world around them. However, computer use should not occur in isolation; teachers and parents should maintain ongoing dialogues to ensure that children are on task and to extend the learning experience through interaction and discovery (Gimbert & Cristol, 2004, p. 208). Haugland (2000b) also found that three- and four-year-old children who use computers show gains in the areas of verbal skills, problem solving, abstraction, intelligence, and long-term memory, as compared to children without computer experience. Thus, it seems safe to say that children with frequent access to quality computer programs will enhance their creativity, critical thinking, and problem-solving skills.

Since the 1980s, studies have demonstrated a high correlation between well-designed instructional programs and cognitive development in children (Pierce, 2004). For example, Apple Classrooms of Tomorrow began experimenting with computer use for classroom instruction in 1985. When changes in pedagogy regarding early literacy caused educators to move toward authentic literacy activities, computers assumed a new role in story reading and writing (Pierce, 2004). Voice-supported reading programs demonstrated significant gains in oral language production, particularly among preschool students with disabilities (Pierce, 2004). Continuing studies indicate that Web use for early literacy development can work—both as a delivery device for quality early learning instruction and practice, and as a tool for authentic communication, voice-supported reading material, voice-recognition fluency, and phonics/phonemic awareness development activities (Blanchard & Oliver, 1999; Calvert, 1999, pp. 178-208; Clark, 1999; Cordes & Miller, 2000; Valmont, 1999; Vogt & Kamil, 1999; Klein, Nir-Gal, & Darom, 2000).

CURRENT WEB ACTIVITIES

Movement toward Web-based early literacy activities—or combinations of Web- and non-Web activities—appears to be gaining momentum. Such programs are, as yet, limited in scope and availability—perhaps only a dozen or so now exist. Nearly all these programs advertise that they are also successful at preparing young children for success in school and are based on scientific research in reading and early literacy, thus meeting the requirements of *No Child Left Behind* (NCLB) legislation.

A number of U.S. education associations have taken proactive positions on the issue of Web use for early literacy. For example, a major responsibility of the National Association of Educators of Young Children (NAEYC) is trying to ensure that Web programs are used appropriately, and follow best practices for young children. The NAEYC recommends that early literacy programs provide an easy method for parents and teachers to evaluate content and appropriateness. It also recommends that software applications be designed to support learners of different abilities in an atmosphere of collaboration and cooperation (NAEYC, 1996).

Comprehensive and Supplemental Programs

Several companies provide comprehensive, Web-based programs for early literacy. For instance, CompassLearning's Odyssey Reading

Curriculum is an NAEYC-correlated, theme-based program for early literacy that features phonemic awareness, phonics, fluency, and comprehension activities. (www.compasslearningodyssey.com). Plato Reading Center offers emergent-literacy activities, including phonemic awareness, alphabet knowledge, letter-sound relationships, story awareness, vocabulary, and comprehension (www.plato.com). In an example of programming with multiple possibilities (comprehensive and supplemental), Riverdeep offers Destination Reading, a program that covers much the same content as Plato and Compass, with a focus on multiple text genres including fiction, non-fiction, poetry, songs, folk tales, and environmental text (http://www.riverdeep.net).

Web-based programs of a more supplemental nature are also available; that is, supplemental in the sense that they are not quite as broad (fewer content areas), deep (fewer examples of content), or elaborate in learning and assessment as their more comprehensive cousins. For example, Early Reading (www.headsprout.com), Imagination Station (www.istation.com), and Let's Go Learn (www.letsgolearn.com) are supplemental in nature and, while not as broad in scope as the comprehensive programs, they do offer the standard menu of phonemic awareness, phonics, fluency, vocabulary, and comprehension in some form or another. In addition to these comprehensive and supplemental programs, a number of Web sites offer opportunities for early literacy activities. Examples include LiteracyCenter.Net and Sylvan Learning (http://bookadventure.com), which seem to concentrate exclusivity on enticing children to read with fun-type activities. Similar examples include Reading Is Fundamental, a non-profit literacy organization that offers a site called *Reading Planet*, which contains reading and writing games as well as online books (http://www.rif.org/readingplanet). Cognitive Concepts, creator of Earobics, offers a game site to foster early literacy skills (http://www.Earobics.com/gamegoo/gooeyhome.html). PBS Kids, in support of its *Between the Lions*, also offers a free site that contains early literacy stories and games (http://pbskids.org).

FUTURE WEB SOLUTIONS

Today, and in the future, the Web offers the promise of solutions for early literacy learning. With one anchor in the home and another in the schools and libraries, the Web can deliver high-quality, literacy learning opportunities for all children. Ongoing work by the Early Childhood Technology Literacy (ECTL) project (http://www.mcps.k12.md.us/

curriculum/littlekids) suggests that Web programs can provide young children with interactions that will boost their literacy development. The project notes that the Web provides children with virtual field trips and reading materials that teachers can download and adjust for vocabulary, font size, and text simplification. ECTL also provides teachers with online professional development and e-mail, allowing peer communication and collaboration. Such efforts are not limited to the United States; for instance, Australia, Scotland, and European Union members are also emphasizing Web and computer use in early literacy education (http://www.ltscotland.org.uk/ngflscotland; http://www.readingonline.org/international/inter_index.asp?HREF=/international/rrq/39_3/; http://www.pjb.co.uk/npl/bp11.htm).

The U.S. government's NCLB publication, *Put Reading First*, provides suggestions on ways that the Web might support emergent literacy activities. One of its most repeated guidelines is that successful programs must be very specifically targeted to each of the five core areas of literacy learning (phonemic awareness, phonics, fluency, vocabulary, and comprehension (http://www.nifl.gov/partnershipforreading/publications/reading_first1.html#top). NAEYC and the International Reading Association (IRA) also offer publications that support literacy learning.

CONCLUSION

Web use for early literacy is just beginning and much needs to be learned. But, rightly or wrongly, Web activities and programs are growing in numbers and, more to the point, in importance. Just as the case with adults and older students, the Web can engender profound changes for early learning. It could mean better communication between school, home, and daycare providers; multimedia programs that support multiple intelligences and learning abilities; young user-friendly activities and a venue for authentic tasks that are both trackable and assessable. In short, the Web could help boost early literacy learning across different family incomes, environments, backgrounds, learning abilities/handicaps, state and school districts, ethnicities, and language abilities.

Early literacy begins years before the start of formal schooling. Children acquire elementary literacy attitudes and abilities in their formative years. Research and common sense suggest that significant learning gaps exist among children when they come to preschool and formal schooling, and that those gaps often persist through high school.

Clearly, the problem is not limited to the United States; countries around the globe are exploring this issue and developing programs to take advantage of the Web's ubiquitous presence and burgeoning popularity.

The Web can be used both as a delivery system for instruction and as a literacy learning environment for all children, regardless of national origin, residence, diversity in background, income, style, and ability–thus supporting the hope that every child around the world can enter formal schooling well on his/her way to becoming a good reader.

REFERENCES

Anderson, G. (2000). Computers in a developmentally appropriate curriculum. *Young Children, 55*(2), 90-93.

Attewell, P., Suazo-Garcia, B., & Battle, J. (2003). Computers and young children: Social benefit or social problem? *Social Forces, 82*(1), 277-296.

Blanchard, J., & Oliver, J. (1999). The family-school connection: Possibilities for technology. In J. Blanchard (Ed.), *Educational computing in the schools: Technology, communication, and literacy* (pp. 65-72). New York: Haworth.

Calvert, S. (1999). *Children's journeys through the information age.* Boston: McGraw-Hill.

Clark, C. (1999). Putting *Highlights for Children* online. In J. Blanchard (Ed.), *Educational computing in the schools: Technology, communication, and literacy* (pp. 39-46). New York: Haworth.

Cordes, C., & Miller, E. (2000). *Fool's gold: A critical look at computers in childhood.* College Park, MD: Alliance for Childhood.

Davis, B., & Shade, D. (1994). *Don't isolate! Computers in the early childhood curriculum.* Champagne, IL: ERIC Clearinghouse on Elementary and Early Childhood Education. (ERIC Document Reproduction Service No. ED 375 991)

Dolowy, B. (2000). Educators share ideas about software for children-Educational tool or inappropriate activity. *Child Care Information Exchange, 136*, 76-78.

Filipenko, M., & Rolfsen, G. (1999). What will it take to get computers into an early childhood education classroom? *Canadian Children, 24*(2), 35-38.

Gimbert, B., & Cristol, D. (2004). Teaching curriculum with technology: Enhancing children's technological competence during early childhood. *Early Childhood Education Journal, 31*(3), 207-216.

Haugland, S. (2000a). *Computers and young children.* Champagne, IL: ERIC Clearinghouse on Elementary and Early Childhood Education. (ERIC Document Reproduction Service No. ED 438 926)

Haugland, S. (2000b). What role should technology play in young children's learning? Part 2. Early childhood classrooms in the 21st century: Using computers to maximize learning. *Young Children, 55*(1), 12-18.

Klein, S., Nir-Gal, O., & Darom, E. (2000). The use of computers in kindergarten. With or without adult mediation: Effects on children's cognitive performance and behavior. *Computers in Human Behavior, 16*(6), 591-608.

National Association of Educators of Young Children. (1996). *Position statement on technology and young children, ages 3 through 8.* Retrieved July 21, 2004, from http://www.naeyc.org/resources/position_statements/pstech98.htm

Nielsen//NetRatings. (2003). *Kids account for one out of five Internet surfers in the U.S.: More than 27 million American kids connect online, according to Nielsen//NetRatings.* Retrieved June 12, 2004, from http://www.nctratings.com/pr/pr_03102.pdf

Pendleton, M. (2001). Becoming a child's advocate for toys–Instead of TV, video games, or computers! *Montessori Life, 13*(2), 10-11.

Pierce, P. (2004). *Technology integration into early childhood curricula: Where we've been, where we are, where we should go.* (Ch. 3). Retrieved June 7, 2004, from Chapel Hill: University of North Carolina. http://idea.uoregon.eduj/~ncite/documents/techrep/tech11-3html.

Poftack, A. (2004). Gleanings. *Technology and Learning, 24*(6), 40.

Put Reading First. (2004). Retrieved July 22, 2004, from http://www.nifl.gov/partnershipforreading/publications/reading_first1.html.

U.S. Census Bureau. (2001). *Home computers and Internet use in the United States, August, 2000.* Special Studies. Retrieved July 21, 2004, from http://www.Census.gov/main/www/cen2000.html.

Vail, K. (2001). How young is too young? *American School Board Journal, 6,* 14-17.

Valmont, W. (1999). Technology: Impact on literacy development. In J. Blanchard (Ed.), *Educational computing in the schools: Technology, communication, and literacy* (pp. 73-78). New York: Haworth.

Vogt, K., & Kamil, M. (1999). Technologies for literacy development. In J. Blanchard (Ed.), *Educational computing in the schools: Technology, communication, and literacy* (pp. 89-92). New York: Haworth.

Wardle, F. (1999). Foundations for learning. How children learn: The latest on ways to maximize children's learning and development. *Children and Families, 18*(3), 66.

Krista Simons
Doug Clark

Supporting Inquiry in Science Classrooms with the Web

SUMMARY. This paper focuses on Web-based science inquiry and five representative science learning environments. The discussion centers around features that sustain science inquiry, namely, data-driven investigation, modeling, collaboration, and scaffolding. From the perspective of these features five science learning environments are detailed: Whyville, WISE, River City, Knowledge Forum, and Biokids. These examples are presented because they represent a wide range of strategies, genres, and goals for science inquiry. While these environments differ from one another in important ways, they do share common features that sustain science inquiry. *[Article copies available for a fee from The Haworth Document Delivery Service: 1-800-HAWORTH. E-mail address: <docdelivery@haworthpress.com> Website: <http://www.HaworthPress.com> © 2004 by The Haworth Press, Inc. All rights reserved.]*

KEYWORDS. Science inquiry, Web-based learning, problem-solving, modeling, scaffolding

KRISTA SIMONS is Assistant Professor, Purdue University, West Lafayette, IN 47909 (E-mail: kds@purdue.edu).
DOUG CLARK is Assistant Professor, Curriculum and Instruction, Arizona State University, Tempe, AZ 85287-0911 (E-mail: dbc@asu.edu).

[Haworth co-indexing entry note]: "Supporting Inquiry in Science Classrooms with the Web." Simons, Krista, and Doug Clark. Co-published simultaneously in *Computers in the Schools* (The Haworth Press, Inc.) Vol. 21, No. 3/4, 2004, pp. 23-36; and: *Web-Based Learning in K-12 Classrooms: Opportunities and Challenges* (ed: Jay Blanchard, and James Marshall) The Haworth Press, Inc., 2004, pp. 23-36. Single or multiple copies of this article are available for a fee from The Haworth Document Delivery Service [1-800-HAWORTH, 9:00 a.m. - 5:00 p.m. (EST). E-mail address: docdelivery@haworthpress.com].

Digital Object Identifier: 10.1300/J025v21n03_04

Conventional wisdom suggests that the adoption of technology innovations in K-12 education is a slow process, and this is also true of the Internet or Web resources. The most recent data available, the NetDay survey of 210,000 students from 3,000 schools (October 25 to November 3, 2003; NetDay, 2003), showed that students do not typically use the Web at school for class work but instead use it at home. At home they are active users of the Web, but the primary use includes games, communication, and not much further. Students understand that the Web can be a powerful learning tool but do not use it as such–especially at school. Not surprisingly, the survey concluded that the potential of the Web is not being realized.

In science education, many researchers have attempted to address the need for students (and their teachers) to move beyond simple Web-based functions like communications or GOOGLE-like information searches and to tap the Web's capacity to teach and enhance learning. They have suggested that Web-based science inquiry environments can sustain meaningful science inquiry activities and ensure effective teaching and learning. To ensure this is possible, science environments have adopted four key features, namely, data-driven investigation, modeling, collaboration, and scaffolding. Why are these features important in Web-based science inquiry environments?

DATA-DRIVEN INVESTIGATION

Data-driven investigation engages students as scientific researchers as they investigate problems by accessing primary-source data and other types of information. Such information includes results of scientific experiments, diagrams, articles, and images. Students can investigate theories and generate hypotheses about a specified phenomenon or problem. As students do so, the data they find can be used as evidence to support their investigation and conclusions. Linking data-driven investigation with online resources represents a natural combination, since the Internet can provide access to information and data.

MODELING

As students investigate and gather data, modeling in e-learning environments can help them manipulate and make sense of the data (Edelson, Gordin, & Pea, 1999; Linn & Hsi, 2000). In the process, modeling and simulation tools can make both scientific ideas and students' thinking about those ideas visible (White & Frederiksen, 1998). The use of modeling in science inquiry may involve an extended process of model construction, model evaluation, and model revision. Modeling may also focus on the presentation of an interactive model. Several prominent researchers in science education have suggested that modeling practices can and should be supported not only in online learning but also across the broader science curriculum (Clement, 1989; Hestenes, 1992; Lehrer & Romberg, 1996; Linn & Hsi, 2000; Roth, 2001; Schauble, Glaser, Duschl, Schulze, & John, 1995; White & Frederiksen, 1998).

COLLABORATION

Collaboration is a central feature in science inquiry activities. As such, it helps engage students in theory construction and problem solving (Blumenfeld, Marx, Soloway, & Krajcik, 1996). It is believed by some researchers that collaboration enhances opportunities for generative learning; that is, students have the opportunity to discuss, explain, and learn (The Cognition and Technology Group at Vanderbilt, 1992). Some researchers have suggested that the primary goals of collaboration are twofold: (a) to activate individuals' prior experience or knowledge in related areas, and (b) to promote clarity into the problem-solving directions the group should take through refining what is not understood (Kelson & Distlehorst, 2000; Schmidt & Moust, 2000; Wilkerson, 1996). Toward these goals, many online environments provide student collaboration opportunities.

SCAFFOLDING

Scaffolding presents students with additional resources to support their inquiry. Scaffolds are tools, strategies, or guides that support students in gaining higher levels of understanding or attaining a skill that would be beyond their reach without this type of guidance (Jackson, Stratford, Krajcik, & Soloway, 1996). Wood, Bruner, and Ross (1976) define effective scaffolding as "controlling those elements of the task that are initially beyond the learner's capability, thus permitting him to concentrate upon and complete only those elements that are within his range of competence" (p. 9). Because Web-based science inquiry environments typically employ a variety of research and problem-solving activities, many include scaffolding.

SCIENCE ENVIRONMENTS

There are five prominent Web-based science environments. They include BioKids (2004), Whyville (2004), WISE (2004), River City (2004), and Knowledge Forum (2004).

BioKids: Kids' Inquiry of Diverse Species

Within the BioKids (2004) environment students participate in a variety of activities related to biodiversity (http://www.onesky.umich. edu/site/biokids.html). Students begin by learning to identify indications of various animal species as well as collecting observations around school. Students then collect data from a wider area. They compare these observations with other findings from the Animal Diversity Web database, focusing on one or two species. Next, students examine patterns both in the observations recorded from their own school and those outside the school. They look for similar or complementary species. In addition, students compare and contrast their results with others. This culminates in a written report on the selected species, which is posted in the online database. Finally, students research within the database to compare and contrast a small number of species in terms of distribution, habitats, behaviors, and other patterns. Part of their comparison involves generating maps, narratives, and predictions that are also added to the database as part of this process (for a more detailed description, see Songer, 2003).

Whyville

Whyville (2004) is an informal science environment (http://www. whyville.net). Whyville is advertising-free and free to use (although there is an optional "fast pass" subscription). Students log onto the site and can participate in a wide range of activities including science activities, chatting, arranging face characteristics for their avatars, and building virtual homes. Whyville is a virtual multi-player community in which students own and construct their own houses and interact with other members of the community.

Whyville contains numerous buildings that support scientific inquiry activities. These activities are, in turn, directly connected to a set of 10-week science curriculum units developed for grades 7 through 12. This curriculum, together with the Whyville environment, spans traditional curriculum areas, linking chemistry, biology, and physics, as well as subjects like the history of science. Thus, Whyville is intended to directly support real classroom teaching and educational innovation, as well as teacher training and home use. The activities and features of the site have made Whyville very popular with students between the ages of 8 and 14. More than 60% of the users are females, which is especially unusual for a science site (Foley, Jones, & McPhee-Baker, 2002). Whyville has a registered user base of more than 300,000, with about 4,000 students visiting daily as of early 2003 (Tynes & Kafai, 2003).

Web-Based Inquiry Science Environment (WISE)

WISE (2004) is an inquiry-based environment that engages students in the intentional process of diagnosing problems, critiquing experiments, distinguishing alternatives, planning investigations, researching conjectures, searching for information, constructing models, debating with peers, and forming coherent arguments about science (http://wise. berkeley.edu). It allows teachers to organize Internet resources into pedagogically useful and appropriate inquiry projects for students. To promote knowledge integration, WISE helps students engage in sustained reasoning, monitor their own progress, and identify new questions and opportunities to apply their knowledge.

To create inquiry projects, students use the (a) WISE Scaffolded Knowledge Integration Framework, (b) WISE features, and (c) WISE authoring language. The authoring language allows students to explore a question, come up with their own perspective, and develop a coherent argument (Clark & Jorde, 2004; Linn, Shear, Bell, & Slotta, 1999). WISE partnerships have created projects on a broad range of topics, including the causes of declining amphibian populations, responses to the worldwide threat of malaria, decisions concerning genetic modification of foods, design of houses for desert climates, design of rainforest investigations, critique of environmental plans, analysis of water quality, and interpretation of conflicting claims about life on Mars. The WISE library includes over 25 projects that have undergone classroom testing and demonstrated an impact on knowledge integration for close to 100,000 students.

Multi-User Virtual Experiential Simulator: River City

River City (2004) is a fictitious, online, nineteenth-century town that students enter as imaginary scientists, or avatars, whose goal is to learn about the town (http://www.gse.harvard.edu/~dedech/muvees/index. htm). Museum photos from the time period are used to illustrate the buildings and street scenes, which include homes, stores, a hospital, and a university. Students visit data collection stations to obtain detailed information about water samples in the area. In addition, students listen to residents' conversations, which convey important clues regarding circumstances in River City. Patterns emerge through the research, such as the fact that more poor people are becoming ill than rich people. Students study these patterns in order to draw conclusions about life in the town.

Students communicate online through a variety of methods, which include chat, the projection of snapshots that communicate individual points of view, a teleport function that allows students to join someone else for joint investigation, and kiosks that allow students to post news items and view maps of the city. This culminates in students composing a letter to the mayor of River City suggesting ways to address the environmental and health concerns of the town (Dede & Ketelhut, 2003).

Knowledge Forum

Knowledge Forum (2004) is a multipurpose virtual workspace designed to sustain the process of building common knowledge around a central problem or theme (http://www.knowledgeforum.com). The theme can relate to any topic, not just those in science. For example, themes include the investigation of the physics of airplane flight, the systems of the human body, the perspectives of the North and the South in the Civil War, and the geometry involved in designing a fountain for a middle school common area.

At the outset, teachers pose an engaging problem or question. Students are responsible for developing responses that present their hypotheses and warrant their assertions. They post their responses through asynchronous discussion and can attach an image, movie, or sound file to their text response. When students read others' responses, they can choose one of two direct response options: build-on or annotate. The build-on feature results in a thread beneath the first message, while the annotate feature allows students to actually insert text into the original message, which may expand on a point or address a misconception.

Knowledge Forum also contains a search tool. Users have the option to insert keywords for their message for more efficient searching. Finally, Knowledge Forum includes a host of additional tools that allow readers to change the sequence of messages, import selected messages into a separate forum for viewing, and link to external online resources.

INQUIRY FEATURES IN SCIENCE ENVIRONMENTS

Each of the five online or Web-based science environments discussed presents unique methods and strategies for engaging in scientific inquiry. What follows is a discussion of the ways in which the strategies (data-driven investigation, modeling, collaboration, scaffolding) are incorporated into each environment.

Data-Driven Investigation

Students investigate problems through accessing data and information in each of these projects. For example, within BioKids, students examine and interpret data from the Animal Diversity Web database to draw conclusions and construct reports. Similarly, in the River City environment, students make recommendations to the mayor based on what they learn from their examination of photographs, artifacts, and reports. The primary difference between the information accessed in BioKids and River City involves BioKids' real-time data and River City's archived data.

Whyville's approach emphasizes the process one goes through to obtain scientific information rather than emphasizing the information itself. Whyville supports kids using computers the way that scientists use computers: for (a) data collection, (b) data visualization, (c) simulation and modeling, and (d) scientific communication. Science activities in this site are open-ended in nature. The simulations can be used in many different ways and the explorations can be pursued in many different directions. Students enter their data and observations directly on the site and communicate their ideas and results with one another. Whyville provides motivation for data collection, sophisticated analysis tools, and community venues for the communication of results.

Similarly, WISE projects allow students to access information and data in an open-ended manner. In WISE, however, the information comes from Web sites around the Internet. The original design philosophy assumed that (a) there are fantastic resources on the Web and (b) these resources are rarely organized or structured in a pedagogically appropriate manner for students. Therefore, a WISE goal is to create an environment that could integrate activity structures, tools, and other scaffolding to help students take advantage of Web resources, such as found in NASA databases or other scientific sites.

Each of the five environments contains unique features that allow students to directly contribute to the overall knowledge base. Work and artifacts produced by students are submitted and become part of the collective knowledge to be accessed, analyzed, and interpreted by others. Within BioKids, students' field-observations are submitted to a central database for other students to examine. In Whyville, a community newspaper allows members to post and discuss news that they find on other sites. Knowledge Forum relies solely on participants' contributed knowledge around a central theme; additional experts and teachers can add to the discussion as deemed necessary to address misconceptions and guide students, but the workspace is generic in that no outside resources are supplied unless generated by the authors of the messages. WISE incorporates a show-and-tell feature that allows students to post and share any of their activities, notes, or journals with a group.

The types of investigation students participate in during their inquiry vary in each of the online environments, but the central purpose remains the same: authentic scientific inquiry. Thus, students analyze information, formulate theories related to a central theme, look for confirming and/or disconfirming evidence, exchange ideas with other groups, refine their ideas, and produce an artifact that represents their final conclusion. While these are not necessarily sequential steps, they characterize the majority of students' actions in the five different online environments. Not only do students participate in authentic scientific investigation, their efforts have a real-world purpose and audience that extend beyond the schools.

Modeling

Modeling problems and solutions is also central to most of the five environments. After students have performed investigations and gathered data, modeling can play a prominent role with data visualization and utilization. In other words, students are prompted to use their data for the purposes of modeling a real-world process or task.

The modeling in Whyville primarily takes the form of simulations that students manipulate to achieve rewards. The most well-known of these tasks is the ice skater simulation in which students arrange the arms and legs of a skater to increase her rate of rotation. In another simulation students pilot a hot air balloon using a burner and purge valve to take advantage of different air currents at each altitude to maneuver the balloon. The students are rewarded for how quickly and accurately they can navigate to their target. In all cases, students work with these simulations to earn game money to buy avatar and house upgrades.

Similarly, a core component of the WISE philosophy focuses on making thinking visible. WISE incorporates several modeling tools including a Casual Modeling tool that allows students to organize static casual models within their projects. In addition, project authors can easily integrate simulations from the Web as well as custom simulations. Finally, modeling tools developed by Concord Consortium (http://pedagogica. concord.org/) also link into WISE projects and connect to the WISE database.

Modeling assumes a different form in BioKids and Knowledge Forum. Rather than representing a process or procedure as in WISE or Whyville, modeling is accomplished through the organization of the database site in BioKids (called MyADW). The MyADW database provides structure for mapping of biodiversity within various regions. In other words, the database that is created becomes the actual model. Likewise, in Knowledge Forum, the contributed messages become the model. However, in contrast to many online discussion forums, the model is not static. Students organize and categorize the messages using tools and online features. Similarly, teachers and external content experts can organize the messages, highlight key concepts, and address misconceptions.

The primary method of modeling in these five environments involves representing students' thinking, either through student interaction with a model embedded in the site or through student creation of models exemplified in products and writings. The goal of the modeling is twofold: (a) students have the opportunity to refine their thinking through the modeling process and (b) they can subsequently receive feedback on their ideas. Feedback might be internal, as in Whyville where students are rewarded for inputting quality information, or feedback might be external, as with Knowledge Forum and WISE where teachers, experts, or both can respond to student-published material. Engaging with these models and visualizations may effectively (a) facilitate cognitive offloading by providing students with an external cognitive aid to reduce the amount of information that needs to be held in working memory while building connections, (b) re-represent problems in a format that facilitates the solutions, and (c) graphically constrain the types of mental models that students can construct.

Collaboration

While modeling represents one way of assisting learners through making their investigations meaningful, collaboration is another essential feature in these five environments. In such contexts, collaboration takes on a variety of formal and informal modes. River City promotes collaboration by suggesting that students work together in small groups to control a single avatar. Students discuss new information and make collaborative decisions based on their discoveries. New modes of collaboration can then be developed to promote collaboration among avatars. Attaining a higher level requires helping other students' avatars through peer mentoring.

Whyville comprises a truly collaborative community of learners. This approach to science education is intended to develop a sense of community and belonging. This approach also maintains that students learn best when they learn together and feel like they belong. At Whyville, science education is interactive and technologically sophisticated, yet still connected to the real world of teachers, students, and classrooms. Whyville has established several innovative modes of collaboration and communication between fellow users. WISE facilitates collaboration and communication through several modes. First, students work in pairs at each computer in a manner similar to River City's projects. Second, many WISE projects incorporate the asynchronous online discussion tool as a standard component. Third, WISE has a show-and-tell tool that allows students to choose portions of their work to share online with the rest of the class. Fourth, WISE includes a group data-gathering tool that allows students to collect data using PDAs. The tool collects, uploads, and compiles the data for all students in the class to use. Fifth, many WISE projects involve in-class collaborations, presentations, and debates as central features of the project structure. Finally, while WISE is online, it is designed to be used in classrooms with the assumption that by freeing the teacher from procedural tasks, the teacher can participate as a coach to scaffold students in conceptual matters.

In BioKids, students collaborate in the research, data-collection, and report-generation processes. Students review and comment on one another's reports. Wider collaboration is promoted through the discussion board. Students post questions based on the patterns they observe and have the opportunity to read and respond to others' questions.

Knowledge Forum focuses entirely on collaborative community construction and representation of knowledge regarding a central theme or question. Students present theories, ideas, and results from their research as they synthesize the online postings of their peers to form coherent responses to problems. Obviously classroom implementation of Knowledge Forum also engages significant face-to-face collaboration.

It is generally believed that collaboration can enhance learning outcomes (Qin, Johnson, & Johnson, 1995; Schmidt & Moust, 2000). Effective use of collaborative inquiry has also been acknowledged by Salomon (1993), who associates the value of collaboration with distributed cognition. In other words, peer support can distribute the work, rather than placing the same cognitive load on each student.

Scaffolding

Taken together, modeling and collaboration represent strategies to support students as they engage with science concepts and inquiry within the five environments. Each of the environments further facilitates this engagement through formalized scaffolding.

The WISE inquiry map on the left side of the screen guides students as they investigate the project topic. The map guides students through activities such as online discussions, argument construction, and modeling of scientific phenomena. The map enables students to work individually and independently on their projects rather than constantly asking the teacher for guidance on what to do next. Reflection notes are steps in an inquiry map where students record their thinking processes. Students can always get hints on how to complete a step or write a note by clicking on a help icon. Additionally, teachers can customize WISE library projects to take advantage of local resources or other information personally relevant to their students.

Similar to the WISE environment, Knowledge Forum presents a variety of scaffolds to assist students in constructing meaningful information posts. For example, students view a message screen when they construct a post. A pull-down menu includes a series of sentence starters students can use to construct their responses. Students can select prompts, and the recommended prompts appear. The scaffolding tools are dynamic, allowing the teacher to develop custom scaffolds or to select from a set of predetermined tools, such as message prompts.

The most important scaffolding in Whyville is the context of the site itself. All students (Whyvillians) can ask one another for help as a part of community conversations. The site also uses simulations as scaffolds. Each simulation includes links to text descriptions of the rules and goals for the simulation. Students can also obtain basic feedback (e.g., students can see their balloons' location change). Occasionally a text message will pop up with some information. In the balloon example, a message pops up when the student runs out of fuel or goes out of bounds.

Scaffolding for students in River City is currently user-reliant. For example, teachers and other users can send messages to students, provide hints or tips to students, or teleport those students' avatars to another location. The student receives a message that another student would like to send a shared view. Upon accepting the request, the student transports and can view the recommended image and information. The developers also hope to create historical and contemporary-leader avatars to guide students. For example, Ellen Swallow Richards, a pioneer in water quality research, is the patron saint of River City. Ellen will actively interact with other avatars in future iterations of River City to provide hints and help students locate essential information.

Scaffolding in these five science environments supports a set of important processes for students and teachers. Saye and Brush (2002) make an important distinction between soft and hard scaffolds. Soft scaffolds are dynamic and represent the timely guidance provided by the teacher during the inquiry process. In contrast, hard scaffolds are static and represent forms of guidance that can be produced in advance based on the developer's expert knowledge and experience (Saye & Brush, 2002). Hard scaffolds might assist students with comprehension of complex concepts or tasks, or they might coach students to think more deeply when they would typically be satisfied with superficial explanations. Thus, both hard and soft scaffolds can provide assistance to students.

CONCLUSION

This discussion has highlighted five science-inquiry environments (Whyville, WISE, River City, Knowledge Forum, and Biokids). For students, the potential learning opportunities in these Web-based environments are exceptional. For teachers, the opportunities are just as exceptional. At no other time in the history of K-12 science education have students and teachers shared such remarkable resources. This optimism is driven by the unique manner in which each of the Web-based environments offers meaningful and authentic teaching and learning activities. In the final analysis, the uses of Web-based data-driven investigation, modeling, collaboration, and scaffolding are just beginning. Tomorrow's uses will be better and better–and hopefully so will tomorrow's science teachers and their young scientists.

REFERENCES

BioKids (2004). [Online]. Available: http://www.onesky.umich.edu/site/biokids.html.

Blumenfeld, P., Marx, R., Soloway, E., & Krajcik, J. (1996). Learning with peers: From small group cooperation to collaborative communities. *Educational Researcher, 25*(2), 27-40.

Clark, D., & Jorde, D. (2004). Helping students revise disruptive experientially-supported ideas about thermodynamics: Computer visualizations and tactile models. *Journal of Research in Science Teaching, 41*(1), 1-23.

Clement, J. (1989). Learning via model construction and criticism. In G. Glover, R. Ronning, & C. Reynolds (Eds.), *Handbook of creativity: Assessment, theory, and research* (pp. 341-381). New York: Plenum.

Dede, C., & Ketelhut, D. (2003, April). *Designing for motivation and usability in a museum-based multi-user virtual environment.* Paper presented at the annual meeting of the American Educational Research Association, Chicago, IL.

Edelson, D., Gordin, D., & Pea, R. (1999). Addressing the challenges of inquiry-based learning through technology and curriculum design. *The Journal of the Learning Sciences, 8*(3,4), 391-450.

Foley, B., Jones, M., & McPhee-Baker, C. (2002, April). *Why girls go to Whyville.net: A girl-friendly online-community for science learning.* Presentation at the annual meeting of the American Educational Research Association, New Orleans, LA.

Hestenes, D. (1992). Modeling games in the Newtonian world. *American Journal of Physics, 60*, 440-454.

Jackson, S., Stratford, S., Krajcik, J., & Soloway, E. (1996). Making dynamic modeling accessible to pre-college science students. *Interactive Learning Environments, 4*(3), 233-257.

Kelson, A., & Distlehorst, L. (2000). Groups in problem-based learning (PBL): Essential elements in theory and practice. In D. Evensen & C. Hmelo (Eds.), *Problem-based learning: A research perspective on learning interactions* (pp. 167-184). New Jersey: Erlbaum.

Knowledge Forum. (2004). [Online]. Available: http://www.knowledgeforum.com.

Linn, M., & Hsi, S. (2000). *Computers, teachers, peers: Science learning partners.* Mahwah, NJ: Erlbaum.

Linn, M., Shear, L., Bell, P., & Slotta, J. (1999). Organizing principles for science education partnerships: Case studies of students' learning about "rats in space" and "deformed frogs." *Educational Technology Research and Development, 47*(2), 61-85.

Lehrer, R., & Romberg, T. (1996). Exploring children's data modeling. *Cognition and Instruction, 14,* 69-108.

NetDay. (2003). *Voices & views from today's tech-savvy students* [Online]. Available: http://www.netday.org/.

Oin, Z., Johnson, D., & Johnson, R. (1995). Cooperative versus competitive efforts and problem solving. *Review of Educational Research, 65*(2), 39-46.

River City: Multi-user virtual experiential simulator: River City. (2004). [Online]. Available: http://www.gse.harvard.edu/~dedech/muvees/index.htm.

Roth, W. (2001). Learning science through technological design. *Journal of Research in Science Teaching, 38,* 768-790.

Salomon, G. (1993). No distribution without individuals' cognition: A dynamic interactional view. In G. Salomon (Ed.), *Distributed cognitions* (pp. 111-138). New York: Cambridge University Press.

Saye, J., & Brush, T. (2002). Scaffolding critical reasoning about history and social issues in multimedia-supported learning environments. *Educational Technology Research and Development, 50*(3), 77-96.

Schauble, L., Glaser, R., Duschl, R., Schulze, S., & John, J. (1995). Students' understanding of the objectives and procedures of experimentation in the science classroom. *Journal of the Learning Sciences 4*(2), 131-166.

Schmidt, H., & Moust, J. (2000). Factors affecting small-group tutorial learning: A review of research. In D. Evensen & C. Hmelo (Eds.), *Problem-based learning: A research perspective on learning interactions* (pp. 19-51). New Jersey: Erlbaum.

Songer, N. (2003, April). *Fostering and measuring the development of complex reasoning in science.* Paper presented at the annual meeting of the American Educational Research Association, Chicago, IL.

The Cognition and Technology Group at Vanderbilt (CTGV). (1992). The Jasper experiment: An exploration of issues in learning and instructional design. *Educational Technology Research and Development, 40*(1), 65-80.

Tynes, B., & Kafai, Y. (2003, April) *Technology and identity: Virtual spaces and objects as mirrors of the self in a large-scale online multi-player science learning community.* Poster presented at the annual meeting of the American Educational Research Association, Chicago, IL.

Web-based Inquiry Science Environment (WISE). (2004). [Online]. Available: http://wise.berkeley.edu.

White, B., & Frederiksen, J. (1998). Inquiry, modeling, and metacognition: Making science accessible to all students. *Cognition and Instruction, 16*(1), 3-118.

Whyville. (2004). [Online]. Available: http://www.whyville.net.

Wilkerson, L. (1996). Tutors and small groups in problem-based learning: Lessons from the literature. In L. Wilkerson & W. Gijselaers (Eds.), *Bringing problem-based learning to higher education: Theory and practice. New directions for teaching and* learning (No. 68, pp. 23-32). San Francisco: Jossey-Bass.

Wood, D., Bruner, J., & Ross, G. (1976). The role of tutoring in problem solving. *Journal of Child Psychology and Psychiatry, 17*(2), 89-100.

Evan Glazer

K-12 Mathematics and the Web

SUMMARY. The Web offers numerous learning resources and opportunities for K-12 mathematics education. This paper discusses those resources and opportunities. Discussion includes (a) asynchronous and synchronous communication tools, (b) the use of data sets to make connections between mathematics concepts and real-world applications, and (c) interactive environments that promote active thinking by allowing students to manipulate mathematical systems, observe patterns, form conjectures, and validate findings. *[Article copies available for a fee from The Haworth Document Delivery Service: 1-800-HAWORTH. E-mail address: <docdelivery@haworthpress.com> Website: <http://www.HaworthPress.com> © 2004 by The Haworth Press, Inc. All rights reserved.]*

KEYWORDS. Math, e-learning, Internet, data, online, modeling, interactive, communication

By 2003, approximately 99% of U.S. schools had access to the Web (NCES, 2003). Consequently, numerous learning approaches have been developed for Web-based K-12 mathematics education. This article will examine how Web resources have been used in mathematics education. Three different approaches will be explored: (a) learning with asynchronous and synchronous communication tools, (b) learning by

EVAN GLAZER is Director, Roanoke Valley Governor's School for Science and Technology, Roanoke, VA 24015 (E-mail: eglazer@rvgs.k12.va.us).

[Haworth co-indexing entry note]: "K-12 Mathematics and the Web." Glazer, Evan. Co-published simultaneously in *Computers in the Schools* (The Haworth Press, Inc.) Vol. 21, No. 3/4, 2004, pp. 37-43; and: *Web-Based Learning in K-12 Classrooms: Opportunities and Challenges* (ed: Jay Blanchard, and James Marshall) The Haworth Press, Inc., 2004, pp. 37-43. Single or multiple copies of this article are available for a fee from The Haworth Document Delivery Service [1-800-HAWORTH, 9:00 a.m. - 5:00 p.m. (EST). E-mail address: docdelivery@haworthpress.com].

Digital Object Identifier: 10.1300/J025v21n03_05

accessing data sets and observing different data analysis methods, and (c) learning in interactive environments.

LEARNING AND COMMUNICATION TOOLS

Communication tools, synchronous and asynchronous, enable students to learn anytime and anywhere. Synchronous communication tools enable students to request help from a teacher or peer without waiting a long time for a response. This form of communication can be effective for online tutoring where two-way communication is continual. In such a setting, synchronous chat rooms encourage students to discuss a problem or idea.

Asynchronous communication tools are valuable when a student would like to reflect on and describe a solution in detail to share with teachers or peers. While there are possibly less exchanges in asynchronous communication, dialogue is often valuable because it allows students to express their solutions. For example, Math Forum's Problem of the Week (http://www.mathforum.org/pow/) challenges students to explore detailed and thought-provoking investigations that often can be solved by multiple methods. Students submit their solutions by e-mail, and then later receive and review a variety of correct solutions from different students.

Research on Problem of the Week math problems (Renninger & Feldman-Riordan, 2000) found that students enhanced their mathematical abilities by developing solutions. This finding was particularly evident for students with lesser mathematical ability. Another finding indicated that students improved their problem-solving strategies as a result. Fetter (2003) noted that the Problem of the Week environment ensured confidentiality and this benefit allowed students to solve problems without being judged.

Frid (2001) studied communication challenges between a group of elementary students and tutors participating in the Number Extravaganza Project. Students' lack of progress in solving problems was attributed to: (a) limitations in the medium to present graphical representations, (b) lack of timeliness in feedback from tutors that prompted independent learning in students, (c) variation in on-site adult supervision, (d) lack of ongoing assessment, and (e) difficulty communicating their reasoning. However, the asynchronous setting allowed students to focus on presentation quality because they were not pressured by a restrictive timeline. For example, students created their own images for their solutions, explained their reasoning from graphs and tables, or incorporated mathematics symbols on their Web pages using HTML (see http://barzilai.org/math%5Fsym.htm) and MathML (see http://www.w3.org/Math/). In terms of creating mathematical symbols, it is important for students to have symbolic software. Without a clear symbolic presentation, the expression and analysis can be misrepresented or misunderstood. Development efforts are now underway to ensure that students will be able to communicate synchronously online with symbolic software (Canessa, 2003).

Online communication tools enable students to collaborate regardless of their location. The Global School House (http://www.gsh.org/) is an international online forum where teachers can develop or join collaborative projects that foster communication. For example, students can collect data in various geographic regions and discuss similiarities and differences in their environments. In an experiment to measure the circumference of the Earth, students can collect data related to the sun's angle of elevation, the time of the day, and the person's latitudinal position on the Earth. Classes of students from similar longitudinal positions on Earth can share this information to predict the angular difference between their cities and then calculate the size of the Earth.

Many online activities requiring communication are multidisciplinary in nature. For example, scientists on world explorations to locations like the Mediterranean Sea, the Galapagos Islands, and the Peruvian rainforest share data they collect with students via satellite and online communication through the JASON project (http://www.jason.org/). The virtual field trip experience gives students an opportunity to explore science, culture, geography, history, and mathematics (Kashner, 2000). Murfin (2001) described such a field trip in the ScienceMOO project with math and science teachers, and outlined an array of innovative online communication tools and applications in development.

In the final analysis, Web-based communication tools have created more learning opportunities. Students can interact with peers around the world, and extend learning beyond their classrooms and schools. Teachers can design projects requiring communication and information exchange unavailable locally. Students can obtain assistance with homework by accessing peers and teachers outside of class time. Online communication tools redefine how, with whom, and when learning occurs.

LEARNING WITH DATA SETS

Access to different types of data is valuable to the study of mathematics. Graphing and function modeling of data can be used to form mathematical connections to realistic phenomena. For example, students can access monthly sunrise and sunset data from thousands of cities in the United States, plot a year's data on a two-dimensional graph, and identify a function that predicts the time of sunrise in the city based on the number of days in the year (http://aa.usno.navy.mil/data/docs/RS_ OneYear.html).

The Internet offers data-sharing resources. Data can be accessed, posted, and updated frequently. For example, real-time data can be obtained on weather patterns, share values in the stock market, and election polls. Teachers can use these resources to assign year-long projects. Students may be required to keep track of patterns, comment on trends, and make predictions about future data.

Access to historic data provides learning opportunities to analyze information and formulate predictions. For example, data from various Olympic events (http://factophile.com/Sports_and_Games/) can be used to devise mathematical models, and predict the year when women will compete with men in the same event. Students interested in purchasing an automobile can predict the value of an automobile using an exponential regression model based on bluebook values (http://www.edmunds.com/used/). They can compare prices in classified ads with their findings to determine whether they are obtaining a fair deal.

Data from the Internet can provide students with problem-solving experiences that promote critical thinking (Glazer, 2001). For example, students can obtain airline, bus, train, and automobile rates to determine when certain modes of transportation are most affordable based on where they live and the desired destination. Online data can be collected to help students predict the price of a home based on multiple factors, such as the size of the land, square footage, number of bedrooms, and age of the home. Students can use these data to purchase a home based on a set allowance.

WebQuests (http://WEBquest.org/) are inquiry-based learning activities that encourage students to collect data and evaluate information to solve problems. WebQuests center around a question for the activity, such as *How should basketball players' salaries be structured?* Students are given procedures, Web resources, and evaluation criteria to put together an answer. Bernie Dodge, the originator of the WebQuest instructional model, claimed student discourse in such activities has potential for meaningful learning experiences (Dodge, 2001). However, Monroe and Orme (2003) found that WebQuest learning experiences varied across gender. For example, girls tended to be cooperative and boys disruptive as they engaged in more thought-provoking discourse. In addition, their findings indicated student discourse to be less conceptually oriented when tasks were procedural in nature.

In summary, the Internet offers new learning opportunities in mathematics with data sets. Students can access real-time data or data difficult to find elsewhere. Consequently, teachers can use Internet-based data to design lessons that involve mathematical modeling and connections to the real world. Since the data are often complex or changing, students can engage in learning experiences with multiple methods and solutions.

LEARNING IN INTERACTIVE ENVIRONMENTS

Interactive learning environments created with Java or ShockwaveTM are prevalent on the Internet in the form of simulations, experiments, and dynamic tools. Simulations are one type of interactive environment where students can explore various mathematical principles in an applied setting. For example, students can examine traffic patterns (http://www.phy.ntnu.edu.tw/java/Others/trafficSimulation/applet.html), airplane noise (http://www.caan.org/footprnt.html), ant colonies (http://polymer.bu.edu/java/java/anthill/Anthill.html), as well as the spread of forest fires (http://www.shodor.org/interactivate/activities/fire1/index.html). In many of the simulations, students can vary independent factors to produce different outcomes. Observing how variations of the independent factors affect a particular environment helps students to connect real-life situations with mathematical concepts. For example, students can observe real-time graphs of a person walking. The independent factors of position, velocity, or acceleration are graphed as a function of time as the direction of the walking person is manipulated. Repeated trials of this simulation enable students to investigate how the graphs change when the variables are modified. As a result, students can describe how the location, speed, and direction of the walker can be identified and calculated from their graph (http://www.mste.uiuc.edu/users/Murphy/MovingMan/MovingMan.html).

Interactive environments provide opportunities for students to run multiple trials of a phenomenon, collect data, and form mathematical conjectures. For example, the cereal box problem (http://www.mste.uiuc.edu/users/reese/cereal/cereal.html) is a mathematical investigation that relies on performing multiple trials to formulate a solution. Students are asked to determine the number of cereal boxes needed to acquire a specified number of prizes. After recording and analyzing multiple trials of data, students can extend their learning by modifying the number of prizes desired and repeating the experiment to generalize their findings.

Probability experiments exist that simulate thousands of coin tosses or rolls of a die to learn the relationship between experimental and theoretical probability (Arbaugh, Scholten, & Essex, 2001). The Monty Hall problem (http://www.shodor.org/interactivate/activities/monty3/index.html) from the television game show *Let's Make a Deal* is another example of an interactive environment. In this activity, students are challenged to find an automobile hidden behind one of many doors. If they do not choose the correct door, they will receive a goat instead of the automobile. In their problem solving, students run multiple trials to develop a door selection strategy, and then explore probability principles to reveal why a particular method is more effective. In addition, students can extend their learning to investigate how the conditions for selecting doors, and chances for winning, might change when more doors are introduced into the problem.

CONCLUSION

The use of Web-based mathematics tools and resources in K-12 classrooms is new and not yet widespread (Li, 2003). But that is changing. More teachers and students are turning to the Web for help and more Web-based tools and resources are under development to help. For example, projects like InterMath (http://www.intermath-uga.gatech.edu/) and the Inquiry Learning Forum (http://ilf.crlt.indiana.edu/) point toward the changes that are coming. Asynchronous and synchronous communication tools, data sets, and interactive mathematics environments are just three uses of Web-based learning. These features–and many more to come–will provide teachers with Web-based instructional tools and resources that promote more active teaching and better learning in mathematics. When that happens, students will develop a better understanding of how mathematics works in the world around them (Jonassen & Reeves, 1996; Morteo & Mariscal, 2003). Quite an accomplishment!

REFERENCES

Arbaugh, F., Scholten, C., & Essex, K. (2001). Data in the middle grades: A probability WebQuest. *Mathematics Teaching in the Middle School, 7*(2), 90-95.

Canessa, E. (2003). E-learning of mathematics. *Proceedings of the ED-MEDIA 2003; World Conference on Educational Multimedia, Hypermedia & Telecommunications, Honolulu, HI, USA,* 1249-1252.

Dodge, B. (2001). FOCUS: Five rules for writing a great WebQuest. *Learning and Leading with Technology, 28*(8), 6-9, 58.

Fetter, A. (2003). Problems of the week engage students with special needs. *ENC Focus,* 10(2). Retrieved July 30, 2003, from http://enc.org/features/focus/archive/special/document.shtm?input=FOC-003143-index

Frid, S. (2001). Supporting primary students' on-line learning in a virtual enrichment program. *Research in Education, 66*(9), 9-27.

Glazer, E. (2001). *Using Internet primary sources to teach critical thinking skills in mathematics.* Westport, CT: Greenwood Press.

Jonassen, D. H., & Reeves, T. C. (1996). Learning with technology: Using computers as cognitive tools. In D. H. Jonassen (Ed.), *Handbook of research for educational communications and technology* (pp. 693-719). Mahwah, NJ: Erlbaum.

Kashner, Z. (2000). Join the cyber caravan! *Instructor, 111*(1), 72-74.

Li, Q. (2003). Would we teach without technology? A professor's experience of teaching mathematics education incorporating the Internet. *Educational Research, 45*(1), 61-77.

Monroe, E., & Orme, M. (2003). *The nature of discourse as students collaborate on a mathematics WebQuest.* Paper presented at the NECC annual conference, Seattle, WA. Retrieved July 30, 2003, from http://ccenter.uoregon.edu/con/necc_ pdf_ upload/necc2003_RP_handouts/MONROE-Orme.pdf

Morteo, G., & Mariscal, G. (2003). *An electronic ludic learning environment for mathematics based on learning objects.* Paper presented at the EDMEDIA annual conference, Honolulu, HI, 849-852.

Murfin, B. (2001). A case study of math and science teacher education in a collaborative virtual learning environment. *Journal of Computers in Mathematics and Science Teaching, 20*(4), 405-425.

National Center for Education Statistics (NCES). (2003). *Internet access in the public schools and classrooms: 1994-2002.* Washington, DC: Author.

Renninger, K., & Feldman-Riordan, C. (2000). The impact of Math Forum's Problem(s) of the Week on students' mathematical thinking. In B. Fishman & S. O'Connor-Divelbiss (Eds.), *Fourth International Conference of the Learning Sciences* (pp. 52-53). Mahwah, NJ: Erlbaum.

Robert H. Lombard

Social Studies and the Web Today

SUMMARY. Social studies educators have identified three areas where the Web is being used to assist social studies teaching and learning: inquiry-based learning, online interaction, and displaying student work online. Examples of each are provided. The chapter concludes with the challenges ahead. *[Article copies available for a fee from The Haworth Document Delivery Service: 1-800-HAWORTH. E-mail address: <docdelivery@haworthpress. com> Website: <http://www.HaworthPress.com> © 2004 by The Haworth Press, Inc. All rights reserved.]*

KEYWORDS. Social studies, inquiry-based learning, online interaction

Technology and social studies education have developed a fickle relationship over the last quarter century. Martorella (1997), for example, described technology as the "sleeping giant in the social studies curriculum" and that "there have been few serious attempts to rouse him" (p. 511). This state of affairs was echoed a few years ago when several colleagues from my doctoral student days were reminiscing on the classroom potential of technology in social studies teaching. During that conversation, one colleague mused that he was "getting a bit tired"

ROBERT H. LOMBARD is Professor of Social Science Education, Department of Curriculum and Instruction, Western Illinois University, Macomb, IL 61455 (E-mail: R-Lombard@wiu.edu).

[Haworth co-indexing entry note]: "Social Studies and the Web Today." Lombard, Robert H. Co-published simultaneously in *Computers in the Schools* (The Haworth Press, Inc.) Vol. 21, No. 3/4, 2004, pp. 45-51; and: *Web-Based Learning in K-12 Classrooms: Opportunities and Challenges* (ed: Jay Blanchard, and James Marshall) The Haworth Press, Inc., 2004, pp. 45-51. Single or multiple copies of this article are available for a fee from The Haworth Document Delivery Service [1-800-HAWORTH, 9:00 a.m. - 5:00 p.m. (EST). E-mail address: docdelivery@haworthpress.com].

of writing that the great potential of technology remained unfulfilled in most social studies classrooms. While I would expect that the conversation would go much the same way if these colleagues were to meet again today, there have been some important developments worthy of discussion.

THE WEB TODAY

In the last few years, educational researchers have begun to investigate the Web and its uses in social studies education. One source of information has been content analysis of publications and national level conference presentations. Simply put, analyses look for entries about Web uses. The assumption is that more entries mean more interest and more use–fewer entries, just the opposite. For instance, Martorella (1997) found, after examining the National Council for the Social Studies and the American Education Research Association annual programs, that there were only a small number of technology-related articles and sessions and no mention was made of the Web. Martorella's conclusion was that this "suggested a critical need for more research, reflection, and development efforts" (p. 512). A few years later, Whitworth and Berson (2002) reported that only four out of 325 articles published from 1996 to 2001 for social studies education involved Web-based use. VanFossen and Shively (2003) drew the same conclusion after a review of National Council for the Social Studies programs (1995-2002). Their review demonstrated a rise in the number and percentage of Web-based oriented sessions from 1995 to 1997 with a plateau until 1999 followed by a decline in 2001 and 2002. VanFossen and Shively (2003) stated in their concluding remarks:

> Believing that the NCSS annual meeting provides a real opportunity for the professional development of social studies teachers, this study began with the question of how Internet sessions at the annual meeting might be reflective of K-12 classroom teachers' apparent desire to be more productive and efficient in their use of the Internet. Our findings that the Internet sessions being presented were relatively few in number, decreasing in proportion, and basic in content gave us pause. (p. 520)

In spite of the lack of interest that could be implied by the analyses just cited, content analysis is just one tool for investigating Web use.

Commentaries are another. For example, Bass and Rosenzweig (2000) offer up their experiences with the American Memory Fellows at the U.S. Library of Congress. In doing so, Bass and Rosenzweig describe three uses they see in today's social studies classrooms, namely, (a) inquiry-based learning, (b) online interaction, and (c) displaying student work online in new formats. A discussion of the three should provide some sense of Web-based social education today.

INQUIRY-BASED LEARNING

An intriguing form of inquiry learning is the WebQuest format developed by Dodge in the mid-1990s at San Diego State University in the United States. A WebQuest is a learning tool that promotes inquiry-oriented activities with information drawn from the Web (Dodge, 2004).

A WebQuest is ideally suited to make inquiry learning work. A clear objective is indicated, and steps to compete the objective are thoroughly laid out. A good WebQuest usually contains Internet links to information sources and sometimes e-mail addresses of people who are experts. As a result, students spend time learning about the objective and not wasting countless hours searching the Internet for the information they need.

WebQuests can be either short- or long-term search activities. Short-term WebQuest activities introduce students to a new topic and help them understand the material. A long-term WebQuest requires students to not only understand new information but to extend what they have learned. For example, students may have to construct a type of lesson plan to teach others about the subject matter. Students are expected to evaluate what they are learning and identify main components of the material. For example, a teacher may create a long-term WebQuest on the American Civil War. The students may be given Internet links about the political positions of the North and South. Another link may contain information on different types of weapons used during that period or strategies used by the Civil War generals. E-mail addresses of Civil War experts may be given to the students to ask questions. Finally, the students may be asked to post their conclusions and opinions of the war on the Internet.

Dodge (2004) believes that the primary objectives of WebQuests are to (a) use learners' time well, (b) focus on using information rather than looking for it, and (c) support learners' thinking at the levels of analysis, synthesis, and evaluation. With or without WebQuests, students are using the Web to gather information, but with WebQuests students are us-ing the Web with a research framework that can be linked to models of active-learning in social studies (see Banks, 1999; Beyer, 1971; Massialas & Cox, 1966). For example, Milson (2002) used WebQuests with sixth-grade students studying ancient Egypt. Milson found that the students changed their perceptions of the Internet after the use of WebQuests and that all students, including those with limited academic abilities, could complete inquiry-oriented investigations.

Another form of inquiry using the Internet is the "Web Inquiry Proj-ect" (WIP) (Molebash, 2002). The WIP presents an open-inquiry activity designed to promote the investigation of topic-related questions gener-ated by the students themselves. Simply stated, the WIP begins with what Molebash (2004) calls a "hook" that "sparks students' interest in the topic with the goal of eliciting inquiry-oriented questions" (p. 227). In addition to the "hook," a typical WIP also consists of six other stages: questions, procedures, data investigation, analysis, findings, and new questions. These seven stages are designed to guide students through a "spiral path of inquiry" involving asking questions, defining procedures, gathering/investigating data, analyzing/manipulating data, reporting findings/ drawing conclusions, and reflecting. WIPs differ from WebQuests in two significant ways: (a) A WIP initially provides students with broad ques-tions like those in a WIP by Luxon, Wilson, and Zizzo (2004): "Do you think you could be president? Can you think like a leader?" (See http://edWeb.sdsu.edu/wip/examples/decision); and (b) students are to engage in the process of historical inquiry without the step-by-step in-structions built into WebQuests.

ONLINE INTERACTION

The possibilities offered by Web-based interaction in the social stud-ies have ranged from the simple to the complex. Simplest, of course, are online versions of what has been traditionally done in social studies classrooms. For example, mock stock market trading simulations have been moved to the Internet. The levels of connectivity for these simula-tions vary. For example, *The Stock Market Game* (2004) from the Foun-dation for Investor Education and the *Arizona Stock Market Simulation (SMS)* (2004) use simulated online trading, while the *Good News Bears Stock Market Project* (2004) offers offline trading.

A more complex example of online interaction is the University of Maryland's award-winning International Communication and Negotiation Simulations (ICONS) (2004), which provides for online research links and computer-mediated negotiations on complex international topics. This site promotes critical thinking and enhanced interactive learning about social studies issues and is available for K-12 classrooms. Another site, *Decisions, Decisions* (Tom Snyder Productions), provides students with online video clips and other resources needed for discussions about current issues.

Another example of online interaction would be the online exhibits provided by an increasing number of museums. While these do not offer the same level of interaction as simulations, there are often provisions for posting personal reactions to the exhibit. *A More Perfect Union: Japanese Americans and the Constitution* from the Smithsonian's American History Museum (2004) would represent this approach.

DISPLAYING STUDENT WORK ONLINE

Imagine the challenges of using a full range of Web-based technologies in order to demonstrate to others what you have learned. Although students at Libby High School had been participating in the Montana Heritage Project since 1995, the 2003 closing of the logging mill allowed them to share the historical perspective of the mill in a significant way with the workers and the rest of the Libby community through the Web (See http://glef.org/php/article.php?id=Art_1048 for examples). Project LINCOL'N (Living in the New Computer Oriented Learning 'Nvironment) (2004) in Springfield, Illinois, has also placed student work online. Details about the project and student work may be found at http://www.springfield.k12.il.us/resources/projlincoln/index.html. Clearly, displaying student work on the Web is now commonplace. But what is not commonplace are studies that examine the impact of Web-displayed work on students' learning, motivation, and participation as active citizens.

CONCLUSION

There is the potential for the Web to serve social studies education. But getting the Web to serve the principles of inquiry-based social studies education may take some time. Unfortunately, there is no time! The Web is in virtually every school in the United States (NCES, 2003) and in millions and millions of U.S. homes. So, while many social studies teachers are cautious and concerned about its use (Will students come to believe everything as factual?), nevertheless, it is here and teachers should learn to use it wisely and to educate their students on how to use it wisely. Social studies teachers would do well to remember the words of H. Wayne Ross:

> We cannot, however, expect a laissez faire approach to technology adoption in education will necessarily produce positive educational experiences. Instead we must be critically aware of the potential downside of e-learning and demand wise use of technology for the collective good. Clearly the potential benefits of e-learning for learners and teachers are great, but what are the trade-offs? How do we employ technology for appropriate educational ends, as opposed to quick-fix pedagogical or budgetary ends? These are not merely technical questions, but questions that should compel us to consider what role we want for technology in our lives and what might be missing in our schools and communities in a machine-dominated age. As learning technologies become more sophisticated so too must our critical assessments of their impact on our lives. (2000, p. 491)

REFERENCES

American History Museum. *A more perfect union: Japanese Americans and the Constitution*. Retrieved April 9, 2004, from http://www.americanhistory.si.edu/perfectunion/experience/index.html

Arizona Council on Economic Education, *Arizona SMS*. Retrieved February 27, 2004, from http://www.arizonasms.com/

Banks, J., & McGee-Banks, C. (1999). *Teaching strategies for the social studies: Decision-making and citizen action* (5th ed.). New York: Longman.

Bass, R., & Rosenzweig, R. (2000). *Rewriting the history and social studies classroom needs, frameworks, dangers, and proposals*. White Papers on the Future of Technology in Education: U.S. Department of Education. Retrieved February 27, 2004, from http://www.air.org/forum/Bass.pdf

Beyer, B. (1971). *Inquiry in the social studies classroom: A strategy for teaching*. Columbus, OH: Merrill.

Dodge, B. (2004) *The WebQuest page: Site overview*. Retrieved March 18, 2004, from http://Webquest.sdsu.edu/overview.htm

Foundation for Investor Education, *The stock market game*. Retrieved February 27, 2004, from http://www.smg2000.org/

Luxon, J., Wilson, E., & Zizzo, G. (2004). *Do you think you could be president? Can you think like a leader?: A Web inquiry project*. Retrieved May 28, 2004, from http://edWeb.sdsu.edu/wip/examples/decision

Martorella, P. (1997). Technology and social studies–or: Which way to the sleeping giant? *Theory and Research in Social Education, 25*(4), 511-514.

Massialas, B., & Cox, B. (1966). *Inquiry in the social studies.* New York: McGraw-Hill.

Milson, A. (2002). The Internet and inquiry learning: Integrating medium and method in a sixth-grade social studies classroom. *Theory and Research in Social Education, 30*(3), 330-353.

Molebash, P. (2002). *Web inquiry project.* Retrieved May 28, 2004, from http://edWeb.sdsu.edu/wip/index.htm

Molebash, P. (2004). Web historical inquiry projects. *Social Education, 63*(3), 226-229.

National Center for Supercomputing Applications. (2004). *Good news bears.* Retrieved February 27, 2004, from http://archive.ncsa.uiuc.edu/edu/RSE/ RSEyellow/gnb.html

National Center for Educational Statistics. (2003). *Internet access in U.S. public schools and classrooms: 1994-2002.* Washington, DC: Author.

Ross, W. (2000). The promise and perils of e-learning. *Theory and Research in Social Education, 28*(4), 482-492.

Tom Snyder Productions. *Decisions, Decisions.* [Online]. Retrieved February 27, 2004, from http://ddonline.tomsnyder.com/

University of Maryland, *ICONS.* Retrieved February 27, 2004, from http://www.icons.umd.edu/pls/staff/Website.simulation_overview?id=2

U.S. Library of Congress. (2003). *American memory: Historical collections for the National Digital Library.* Washington, DC: Author. Retrieved February 27, 2004, from http://memory.loc.gov/

VanFossen, P., & Shively, J. (2003). A content analysis of Internet sessions presented at the National Council for the Social Studies Annual Meeting, 1995-2002. *Theory and Research in Social Education, 31*(4), 502-522.

Whitworth, S., & Berson, M. (2002). Computer technology in the social studies: An examination of the effectiveness literature (1996-2001). *Contemporary Issues in Technology and Teacher Education, 2*(4), 471-508.

Lucinda Ray
Kimberly Atwill

The Web and Special Education

SUMMARY. This paper details the use of the Internet by educators and parents of students with disabilities, software tools that make the Internet accessible to students with special needs, and the state of Web-based instruction for these students. Issues are discussed that relate to current research with students with various disabilities as well as the scarcity of research with special education students using the Internet. *[Article copies available for a fee from The Haworth Document Delivery Service: 1-800-HAWORTH. E-mail address: <docdelivery@haworthpress.com> Website: <http://www.HaworthPress.com> © 2004 by The Haworth Press, Inc. All rights reserved.]*

KEYWORDS. Special education, assistive technology, disabilities, inclusion, mainstream, adaptive, accessibility, assessment, literacy, individual educational plan (IEP), uses of technology in special education

While all areas of education have been impacted by technology, arguably its most profound impact has been with special education teach-

LUCINDA RAY is Director of Curriculum Development with IntelliTools, Inc., Petaluma, CA 94954 (E-mail: lray@intellitools.com).
KIMBERLY ATWILL is a doctoral student, Educational Psychology Department, Arizona State University, Tempe, AZ 85287-0611 (E-mail: kimberly.atwill@asu.edu).

[Haworth co-indexing entry note]: "The Web and Special Education." Ray, Lucinda, and Kimberly Atwill. Co-published simultaneously in *Computers in the Schools* (The Haworth Press, Inc.) Vol. 21, No. 3/4, 2004, pp. 53-67; and: *Web-Based Learning in K-12 Classrooms: Opportunities and Challenges* (ed: Jay Blanchard, and James Marshall) The Haworth Press, Inc., 2004, pp. 53-67. Single or multiple copies of this article are available for a fee from The Haworth Document Delivery Service [1-800-HAWORTH, 9:00 a.m. - 5:00 p.m. (EST). E-mail address: docdelivery@haworthpress.com].

ers and students (Blackhurst & Edyburn, 2000; Jeffs, Morrison, Messenheimer, Rizza, & Banister, 2003; see also *Journal of Special Education Technology* for discussions). As recently as 30 years ago, special education students were isolated in special schools with minimal educational expectations or hope (Behrmann, 1998). In the United States, passage of the Education for All Handicapped Children Act (1975: P.L. 94-142) and the subsequent follow-up legislation (ADA, 1990; IDEA, 1991, 1997) has challenged educators from all disciplines to re-evaluate the goal of education for special education students. Students who had previously been excluded from schools in the United States have been shifted to mainstream classrooms. As defined by U.S. federal law, special education means specially designed instruction, at no cost to the parents, to meet the unique needs of a child with a disability. It is an umbrella of instructional services that enables students to successfully learn (for U.S. see Section 504 of the Rehabilitation Act, 1973; Education for All Handicapped Children Act, 1975; Americans with Disabilities Act [ADA], 1990; Technology-Related Assistance for Individuals with Disabilities Act, 1988, 1994; Individuals with Disabilities Education Act [IDEA], 1991, 1997).

Today, a vast array of technology-based assistive and adaptive devices allow access to learning opportunities that were previously inaccessible. However, while these technologies are designed to level the classroom playing field for special education students, they are not designed as resources for *enhanced* learning. The notable exception, of course, is technology use with gifted or talented students (Banbury, Walker, & Punzo, 1990; Beasley, 1985). While technology-based assistive and adaptive devices are needed to fully participate in classroom learning, the devices are equally important in using the Web. The adaptations are needed because according to the U.S. Web-based Education Commission Report (2000), nearly 60% of people with disabilities have never even used a personal computer–almost a requirement to use the Web! That percentage may have risen since 2000, but still stands as a stark reminder that using the Web requires adaptations for those with disabilities.

WEB-USE ADAPTATIONS

Special education teachers are likely to serve students with both physical and cognitive disabilities. Providing learning opportunities for these students has always been a challenge. To deal with these challenges, technology has been used as an adaptive or assistive tool. For example, to make a fractions lesson accessible to a student with low vision, physical manipulatives such as fraction bars have been used. To make the fraction problems easier to see, text enlargers have been used. For a student who can see the fractions but cannot use manipulatives, special devices have been used. For students with learning disabilities, teaching fractions has been improved by CAI that can (a) divide the fractional problem into smaller component parts, (b) provide instruction on the parts, and (c) provide auditory and visual cues with lots of supportive feedback.

Over the last three decades, special educators have embraced a variety of technologies designed to help their students (for a review of early efforts, see Goldenberg, Russell, Carter, Stokes, Sylvester, & Kelman, 1984). Many of these adaptations will be needed for Web use. Here are only a few that apply to Web use:

- FM receivers and adapted software for students with hearing impairments.
- Screen enlargers and screen readers for students with low vision.
- Alternative keyboards for students with motor limitations or cognitive limitations.
- Text-to-speech and speech-recognition software for students with low vision, cognitive, or motor limitations.
- Switch devices for students with extremely limited motor skills so they can scan and interact with the content of computer screens.
- Augmentative communication devices for students who cannot speak.
- Software specifically designed to provide multisensory learning environments for students with a variety of learning disabilities and special needs.
- Software developed with Universal Design principles, so that access for users with disabilities is built into the software. Software incorporating these design principles enables all students to work together on the same curriculum and access the same resources.

To use the Web, special educators may need to combine a variety of these technologies and others to ensure success for their students.

WEB SITES FOR TEACHERS AND PARENTS

The Web or Internet provides three important categories of resources that can expand the world of learning for students with special needs.

- First, numerous Web sites for special educators guide teachers in their task of adapting existing materials or discovering new techniques to aid their students. These sites provide downloadable lesson plans, activities, and strategies for adapting curriculum. Listservs encourage teachers to network and share expertise.
- Second, there are online tools that enable students to access materials, either directly online, or by enhancing their computers with adaptive software and direct access to the Internet.
- Third, there are a growing, though still small, number of sites that offer curriculum support particularly appropriate for students with special needs.

Here is a sampling of some of the many Web sites that provide support for teachers and parents of students with special needs. Because Web sites come and go quickly, if a Web address suggested here is no longer active, be sure to try relocating the site via an Internet search engine.

Microsoft's http://www.microsoft.com/enable/at/types.aspx is a Web site that provides a wealth of information about assistive-technology products available for students with hearing, language, learning, mobility, and visual impairments.

SeriWEB.com is the site of special education resources on the Internet. This site provides many links with resources for parents and teachers.

IBM Accessibility Center (www.ibm.com/able/) lists products and software that help people with special needs use technology. For example, IBM offers a talking Web browser (Home Page Reader) and an auditory and phonics program for young children. A number of the available products offer downloadable, free trial versions.

For parents, specialchildren.about.com provides information about a variety of disabilities, including autism, Down syndrome, and cerebral palsy. This site also includes online forums where parents can communicate with one another online, educational resources, games, and suggested adaptations of the resources for students with special needs.

Very Special Home Pages (www.edbydesign.com/gallery/) is a site for families of students with special needs. Parents and students can set up a student's personal home page that can include a biography written by the student's parent or caregiver.

For teachers and parents of young children, www.mcps.k12. md.us/curriculum/pep/pz.html includes many activities, links to other preschool special education sites, and downloadable activities for both regular or special education preschoolers.

Outside the Box! (adhd.kids.tripod.com/) is for both teachers and parents of special needs students. It offers links to many curriculum sites in all subject areas.

THE QIAT listserv (QIAT@LSV.UKY.EDU), Quality Indicators for Assistive Technology, provides a forum for all interested people to participate in discussions focused on the identification and implementation of quality indicators for assistive-technology services for people with disabilities in school settings.

Closing the Gap (www.closingthegap.com) highlights hardware and software products appropriate for people with special needs and explains how this technology is being implemented in education, rehabilitation, and vocational settings around the world. The in-depth articles, product reviews, and extensive product guide offer a variety of resources that help solve technology implementation problems today. Closing the Gap Forums (www.closingthegap.com/forums/) is a discussion board exploring the many ways that technology is being used to enhance the lives of people with special needs. Over 2,300 members participate in the many moderated discussions led by experts in the field.

WEB-BASED TOOLS

Software tools enable users to make customized changes to the user's computer environment, such as increasing font size or color, having text read aloud, providing easier access to menus, or providing assistance through word prediction. Here is a sampling of some of the tools that provide access to the Internet for students with special needs.

Kurzweil Educational Systems (www.kurzweiledu.com) is a leading developer of reading technology for people with learning difficulties and those who are blind or visually impaired. Kurzweil 3000 software uses a multisensory approach–presenting printed or electronic text on the computer screen with added visual and audible accessibility. The product incorporates a host of dynamic features including powerful decoding, study skills, writing and test-taking tools designed to adapt to each individual's learning style and to minimize frustration for both the learner and educator. Kurzweil 3000 provides both audible and visual accessibility to Web pages and allows the search and retrieval of over ten thousand online books. Students now have a sense of freedom to do research projects and reports as well as download contemporary and classic literature. Teachers find that students using Kurzweil 3000 can read the Web and contribute equally with their peers.

Freedom Scientific (www.freedomscientific.com) describes their mission as developing, manufacturing, and marketing innovative technology-based products and serving those with vision impairments and learning disabilities. Their WYNN 3 software transforms printed text into the spoken word. This literacy software tool, designed to enhance success for individuals with reading challenges and writing difficulties, highlights text as it is spoken aloud, increasing reading comprehension. A customizable e-mail system that incorporates the same highlighting and read-aloud features is built in, providing students with an accessible way to use this important feature of the Internet.

RJ Cooper and Associates (www.rjcooper.com), who make software and hardware for persons with special needs, has a simple, but powerful, full-screen, talking e-mail program, ICanEmail. It is designed for those with cognitive challenges, visual challenges, as well as physical challenges. For the user, the program operates in a sequential manner, asking one question at a time, such as Who would you like to send this to? or If you'd like to speak your message, you can do that here. No reading is necessary because the program speaks and reads. The e-mail "partner" (the recipient or sender) sends and receives mail without any special software at all. To him/her it is just like e-mailing with anyone else. Users can access standard e-mail programs through a third-party program. ICanEmail works with keyboard (IntelliKeys, BigKeys), or a pointing device (Magic Touchscreen, SAM-Joystick, SAM-Trackball), or CrossScanner for single switch. There is even an option to operate ICanEmail by voice, even the voice of an augmentative communication device.

CAST, the Center for Applied Special Technology, is a not-for-profit, education research and development organization that works to create opportunities for all students, especially those with disabilities, by using technology to make education more flexible and accessible (www.cast.org). The CAST eReader combines the most powerful features of talking and reading software to make text more accessible to struggling readers and students with disabilities. Available in both Windows and Macintosh versions, eReader adds spoken voice, visual highlighting, and document or page navigation to any electronic text, including the Internet, word-processing files, and scanned or typed-in text.

TextHELP's Browsealoud (www.texthelp.com) is a Web site speech-enabling service that makes Web content accessible to anyone with reading difficulties. It is designed to be simple for users, requiring only a short download of the free program. Browsealoud not only speech enables Web site content, it also speech enables the menus and hyperlinks to ease navigation of the Web site. Users have a choice of voice, pitch, and speed. Simply by scrolling a mouse over the text to be read, Browsealoud will speak the text that is requested, helping to navigate Web sites more easily. TextHELP also makes Read and Write Gold, a software solution for reading and writing needs, bringing comprehensive literacy support through a unique set of features such as word prediction and speech input for the user with literacy or learning difficulties.

Scansoft's (www.scansoft.com/naturallyspeaking) Dragon Naturally Speaking family of products is the fast, easy, and accurate way to turn speech into text. Users can dictate into virtually any Windows-based application, carrying out tasks such as sending e-mail and browsing the Web, at speeds up to 160 words per minute and achieve higher levels of accuracy than ever before. Dragon NaturallySpeaking delivers significant benefits to users who have difficulty using a standard or alternative keyboard. It meets Section 508 standards, established by the U.S. government to make software accessible for people with disabilities.

IntelliTools (www.intellitools.com) is the developer of an alternative keyboard called IntelliKeys, designed for users with limited fine motor skills. IntelliKeys includes a special overlay that provides mouseless access to the Internet. This keyboard is being used in libraries across the United States as well as the United Kingdom.

WEB-BASED INSTRUCTIONAL CURRICULUM

A growing number of curriculum activities have Web capabilities ranging from individual learning activities to complete delivery of curriculum.

Scientific Learning's Fast ForWord family of products (www.scientificlearning.com) is targeted to special education, English Language Learners (ELL), and students at risk. Each product's interactive exercises integrate a proprietary CD-ROM and Internet technology to create an optimal learning environment that adapts to the level of each student. Patented Web-based tracking tools provide ongoing monitoring of each student's progress. For example, Fast ForWord Language software is an Internet and CD-ROM product that develops the fundamental language skills that are the building blocks for reading success, focusing particularly on auditory discrimination. An online assessment tool provides a set of measurement tools to help parents and educators evaluate phonemic awareness and language and reading skills. Progress Tracker, an Internet-based monitoring tool, provides student information for teachers and clinicians.

Reading Upgrade and Comprehension Upgrade, created by Learning Upgrade (readingupgrade.com), are Web-based courses for struggling readers. Students complete all their work online. Other than a standard Internet browser, no special software is needed on the local computer. Reading Upgrade is designed for special needs, Title I, and ESL students from ages eight through adult who are reading at grade 0-grade 5. Comprehension Upgrade, for those reading at grade 4 or higher, teaches students to read and understand textbooks, literature, instructions, directions, and a wide variety of text. It includes techniques like story maps, K-W-L charts, and flow charts to help students analyze what they read. Reading Upgrade and Comprehension Upgrade combine to make a complete one-semester intervention.

Letsgolearn.com (LGL) is a site geared toward both schools and home schooling. It provides an online assessment tool, the Diagnostic Reading Assessment for grades K-12. The assessment tool examines six subskills of reading to gather an accurate picture of the learner's abilities. In addition, the assessment report provides tangible instructional suggestions to begin customized reading instruction. Their Unique Reader product is an individualized reading instruction system that is completely Web-based. It uses the LGL reading assessment to create a custom lesson plan unique to each student. The reading instruction includes over 600 online activities spanning critical areas of the U.S. No Child Left Behind Act. Online lessons are selected based on each student's unique reading profile and utilize a multisensory instructional approach.

Sylvan Learning, a nationally franchised network of tutoring centers, also has an online presence at esylvan.com. Sylvan Learning services are aimed at regular education students who require additional support. However, they also emphasize the benefits their online division provides for troubled students. eSylvan's Skills Assessment, an online diagnostic tool, pinpoints a student's skill gaps. The assessment is used to develop a remedial program specifically tailored to the child's needs. eSylvan offers live, Web-based tutoring through a proprietary online classroom which provides real conversations in real time over the

Internet, using special voice technology that allows student and teacher to have a two-way audio dialogue using a special headset connected to a home PC, much like using a telephone. The student and teacher also write questions and answers to each other in real time, which are displayed on both the student's and teacher's computer screens, along with the eSylvan-designed reading or math lessons. Currently, eSylvan offers the following personalized online programs: Math Essentials for students in grades 3-8, and Academic Reading for students in grades 4-9.

SNOW is the acronym for Special Needs Opportunity Windows, an online community for special education hosted by the University of Toronto (http://snow.utoronto.ca/snowkids). SNOW Kids Web site is a children's portal. The children's portal enables children with special needs to electronically access curriculum. The SNOW Kids Web site provides homework support, online classes, and messages. There is an online library for students who are blind. The SNOW Kids Web site also offers accessible online educational activities.

Tom Snyder's Reading for Meaning (www.tomsnyder.com) is a software program that installs on a local computer, targeted for students in grades 3-8 who need to improve their reading skills. Through explicit modeling and guided practice, students develop skills in five key areas: main idea, inference, sequence, cause and effect, and compare and contrast. The program is also available on an Internet subscription basis.

WEB-BASED RESEARCH

Given that computer technology follows Moore's Law of exponential development, the scarcity of research utilizing these recent technological advances is not surprising. The hardware and software change so rapidly that the laborious nature of educational research cannot keep pace. The Internet is so new that there has been little or no systematic research into the success of Web-based instruction as an academic construct with special education students at any level. The U.S. Department of Education's Institute of Educational Sciences has launched a multi-million-dollar investigation of Web-based reading programs (2003), but there is no mention whether special education students will necessarily be included in any of the study groups. There is hope; the Office of Special Education Programs (OSEP) in the U.S. Department of Education has funded a four-year research institute to investigate the implementation and effectiveness of assistive technology as proposed by the

1997 amendments to IDEA. The University of Kentucky is now host to the newly formed National Assistive Technology Research Institute (http://natri.uky.edu) and should be a quality resource for research and information (Lahm, Bausch, Hasselbring, & Blackhurst, 2001).

Years of learning research would predict, however, that all students, with proper guidance, could benefit from a learner-centered, multi-modal instructional tool (National Center for Educational Statistics [NCES], 2002; Tindall-Ford, Chandler, & Sweller, 1997). The Internet and Web-based instructional media have the potential to allow all students to achieve beyond traditional experiences and expectations. In addition, experts in the field predict that special education students may benefit more than any other sub-group (Hasselbring, 1994; Okolo, Bahr, & Rieth, 1993; Rose & Meyer, 2001). These same experts, however, warn that the Internet and Web-based instruction are merely more sophisticated sources of information with no intrinsic ability to teach (Hasselbring, 1994; Okolo et al., 1993; Rose & Meyer, 2001; Winn, 1997).

Learning Disabilities

Learning disabilities is a relatively new term (Tanner, 2001). Over the past 20 years, educators' knowledge of learning disabilities has increased as has the number of students identified to have these cognitive challenges (Kavale & Forness, 1998). A major thrust of assistive technology in the area of learning disabilities has been providing support for mainstream instruction (Jeffs et al., 2003). Initially, computer-assisted instruction (CAI) focused on drill and practice to build or remediate skills. As educational designers began to understand how computers could be used to create effective learning environments to meet the needs of students who have learning disabilities, the idea of hypermedia was introduced. Research has since documented the benefit for mainstreamed students with learning disabilities of using CAI and hypermedia to support classroom curricula (Boone & Higgins, 1993; Hasselbring, Goin, & Wissick, 1989; Higgins & Boone, 1990; Higgins, Boone, & Lovitt, 1996).

Developmental Disabilities

Different from students who have learning disabilities, the teaching of students who have developmental disabilities has been transformed by the introduction of interactive computers and accompanying software (Jeffs et al., 2003). Early efforts focused on the acquisition of basic skills. However, current technology has been used (a) to improve communication, (b) to provide an alternative means of producing classwork, and (c) to teach life-skills. For example, research has investigated the benefit of virtual shopping via videotape and photographs with positive results (Langone, Shade, Clees, & Day, 1999; Mechling, Gast, & Langone, 2002). Using this instructional methodology as a starting point, well-constructed streaming video via the Internet has the potential to transport students to virtual destinations throughout the city or around the world (Langone, Clees, Rieber, & Matzko, 2003).

Deafness and Hearing Impairments

The systematic implementation of technology with students who have hearing impairments has two sources: (a) auditory access and (b) classroom instruction methodology. Auditory access has progressed along two pathways–amplification devices and sound-to-text translators. Most classrooms in the United States can accommodate the needs of a student who is deaf or has a hearing impairment through a sign language interpreter, real-time captioning, closed captioning, FM system, and/or personal amplification device. When computers first entered classrooms, software programs were specifically intended to be used by students who are deaf or have hearing impairment. A majority of these programs focused on language development. In time, instructional methodologies that were successful in classrooms for those with hearing impairments were integrated into software programs across the curriculum. These programs were similar to those used with children with learning disabilities; a hypermedia format was employed to present an array of resources easily accessed by the student users. One program included printed text, sign language images, and visual image links (Volterra, Pace, Pennacchi, & Corazza, 1995). This approach brought dramatic learning in the one unit developed but was time consuming to create. With the inception of the Internet and Web-links, this type of program is more achievable through a Web-based learning environment. More recently, schools for those with hearing impairments are accessing Web sites created as support for regular education students (and teachers) and the site sponsors are working to make sites equally accessible (coxednet.org).

Visual Impairments

Perhaps the teachers most actively concerned about Web-based accessibility are those involved with students who have visual impairments. Students with visual impairments are mainstreamed at a higher percentage rate than any other special education subgroup (NCES, 2002). As a result, schools have been forced to provide equally accessible curricular materials. Often these materials are Braille texts that are large and arrive chapter by chapter, or audio tape recordings of textbook pages, a medium that can be difficult for the user to manipulate. More recently, the nonprofit organization that creates accessible books, Recording for the Blind and Dyslexic, has been translating texts into a digital sound and text format that is more easily manipulated by users with visual impairments (Sargent, 1998). While the educational benefit of user-friendly audio books is clear for students with visual impairments, researchers have found that special education students with varying forms of mild impairments also benefit from this accommodation (Boyle, Rosenberg, Connelly, Washburn, Brinckerhoff, & Banerjee, 2003; Stahl & Aronica, 2002). But what does this mean for Web use? How can the Web help students with visual impairments? The answer is the same for all special education students! In their article summarizing 20 years of technology in special education, Jeffs et al. (2003) suggested that the power of technology "does not necessarily lie in the development and implementation of new technologies, but in the proper and full implementation of current technologies" (p. 136). The Web is here and Web-based educational opportunities are expanding. To tap into those opportunities, adapted Web-based technologies are needed (Opitz, 2002). Several years ago, Brusilovsky (2000) and Brusilovsky, Eklund, and Schwarz (1998) proposed a union of intelligent tutoring and hypermedia to create "adaptive hypermedia." This media could adapt itself to meet the special needs of each and every user. There are numerous reasons why technology is not better utilized with special education students, including expense and lack of teacher training (Derer, Polsgrove, & Rieth, 1996; Harkins, Loeterman, Lam, & Korres, 1996; Heaviside, Rowand, Hurst, & McArthur, 2000). As Web-based educational opportunities continue to grow, society has a responsibility to not leave behind those who may most benefit from the flexibility and power it can provide.

CONCLUSION

Each subgroup of special education students has a history long and wide of using technology as a bridge to access instruction. The future, however, is not in maintaining and maximizing the benefits for individual groups, but in capitalizing on the malleability, constructability, and variety of instructional opportunities that the Web can provide. All people with disabilities can benefit from well-designed computer-assisted instruction (Christmann, Badgett, & Lucking, 1997; Scherer, 2003). More than 10 years ago, Hasselbring (1994) called for a dramatic change in the approach and design of what he called "integrated media." Writing in a special issue of the *American Annals of the Deaf*, Hasselbring exhorted educators to "break the mold of existing curricula and [to] fundamentally alter the relationship among teacher, learner, and the tools for teaching and learning" (p. 36). Whether the future holds "integrated media," "adaptive hypermedia," or something else not foreseen, hopefully it holds more opportunities for special education teachers and students to use the Web for learning.

REFERENCES

Banbury, M., Walker, H., & Punzo, R. (1990). Thinking cap: A computer art program for gifted & talented students. *Gifted Child Today, 13*, 32-35.

Beasley, W. (1985). The role of microcomputers in the education of the gifted. *Roeper Review, 7*(3), 156-159.

Behrmann, M. (1998). Assistive technology for young children in special education. In *Yearbook (Association for Supervision and Curriculum Development)* (pp. 73-93). Alexandria, VA: Association for Supervision and Curriculum Development.

Blackhurst, A., & Edyburn, D. (2000). A brief history of special education technology. *Special Education Technology Practice, 2*, 21-36.

Boone, R., & Higgins, K. (1993). Hypermedia basal readers: Three years of school-based research. *Journal of Special Education Technology, 12*(2), 86-106.

Boyle, E., Rosenberg, M., Connelly, V., Washburn, S., Brinckerhoff, L., & Banerjee, M. (2003). Effects of audio texts on the acquisition of secondary-level content by students with mild disabilities. *Learning Disability Quarterly, 26*(3), 203-214.

Brusilovsky, P. (2000). Adaptive hypermedia: From intelligent tutoring systems to Web-based education. Retrieved March 24, 2004, from http://www.sis.pitt. edu/~peterb/papers/ITS00inv.html

Brusilovsky, P., Eklund, J., & Schwarz, E. (1998). Web-based education for all: A tool for development adaptive courseware. *Computer Networks and ISDN Systems, 30*, 291-300.

Christmann, E., Badgett, J., & Lucking, R. (1997). Microcomputer-based computer-assisted instruction within differing subject areas: A statistical education. *Journal of Educational Computing Research, 16*(3), 281-296.

Derer, K., Polsgrove, L., & Rieth, H. (1996). A survey of assistive technology applications in schools and recommendations for practice. *Journal of Special Education Technology, 13*(2), 62-80.

Goldenberg, E., Russell, S., Carter, C., Stokes, S., Sylvester, M., & Kelman, P. (1984). *Computers, education and special needs.* Reading, MA: Addison-Wesley.

Harkins, J., Loeterman, M., Lam, K., & Korres, E. (1996). Instructional technology in schools educating deaf and hard of hearing children: A national survey. *American Annals of the Deaf, 141*(2), 59-65.

Hasselbring, T. (1994). Using media for developing mental models and anchoring instruction. *American Annals of the Deaf, 139*, 36-43.

Hasselbring, T., Goin, L., & Wissick, C. (1989). Making knowledge meaningful: Applications of hypermedia. *Journal of Special Education Technology, 10*(2), 61-72.

Heaviside, S., Rowand, C., Hurst, D., & McArthur, E. (2000). *What are the barriers to the use of advanced telecommunications for students with disabilities in public schools?* Washington, DC: National Center for Educational Statistics. (ERIC Document Reproduction Service No. ED439535)

Higgins, K., & Boone, R. (1990). Hypertext computer study guides and the social studies achievement of students with learning disabilities, remedial students, and regular education students. *Journal of Learning Disabilities, 23*(9), 529-540.

Higgins, K., Boone, R., & Lovitt, T. (1996). Hypertext support for remedial students and students with learning disabilities. *Journal of Learning Disabilities, 29*(4), 402-412.

Jeffs, T., Morrison, W., Messenheimer, T., Rizza, M., & Banister, S. (2003). Retrospective analysis of technological advancements in special education. *Computers in the Schools, 20*(1/2), 129-152.

Kavale, K., & Forness, S. (1998). The politics of learning disabilities. *Leaning Disability Quarterly, 21*(4), 245-273.

Lahm, E., Bausch, M., Hasselbring, T., & Blackhurst, A. (2001). National Assistive Technology Research Institute. *Journal of Special Education Technology, 16*(3), 19-25.

Langone, J., Clees, T., Rieber, L., & Matzko, M. (2003). The future of computer-based interactive technology for teaching individuals with moderate to sever disabilities: Issues relating to research and practice. *Journal of Special Education Technology, 18*(1), 5-16.

Langone, J., Shade, J., Clees, T., & Day, T. (1999). Effects of multimedia instruction on teaching functional discrimination skills to students with moderate/severe intellectual disabilities. *International Journal of Disability, Development and Education, 46*(4), 493-513.

Mechling, L., Gast, D., & Langone, J. (2002). Computer-based video instruction to teach persons with moderate intellectual disabilities to read grocery aisle signs and locate items. *The Journal of Special Education, 35*(4), 224-240.

National Center for Educational Statistics. (2002). *Digest of educational statistics 2002.* Washington, DC: U.S. Department of Education.

Okolo, C., Bahr, C., & Rieth, H. (1993). A retrospective view of computer-based instruction. *Journal of Special Education Technology, 12*(1), 1-27.

Opitz, C. (2002). The effects of implementing Web accessibility standards on the success of secondary adolescents with learning disabilities. (Doctoral dissertation, Arizona State University, 2002). *Dissertation Abstracts International, 63*(11A), 3919.

Rose, D., & Meyer, A. (2001). *The future is in the margins: The role of technology and disability in educational reform.* Retrieved April 17, 2004, from http://www. air.org/forum/AbRose_Meyer.htm

Sargent, M. (1998). *Digital textbooks.* Retrieved March 27, 2004, from http:// www.glef.org

Scherer, M. (2003). *Connecting to learn: Education and assistive technology for people with disabilities.* Washington, DC: American Psychological Association.

Stahl, S., & Aronica, M. (2002). Digital text in the classroom. *Journal of Special Education Technology, 17*(2), 57-59.

Tanner, D. (2001). The learning disabled: A distinct population of students. *Education, 121*(4),795-798.

Tindall-Ford, S., Chandler, P., & Sweller, J. (1997). When two sensory modes are better than one. *Journal of Experimental Psychology: Applied, 3*(4), 257-287.

U. S. Department of Education, Institute for Education Sciences. (2003). *Identifying and implementing educational practices supported by rigorous evidence: A user friendly guide.* Washington, DC: Author.

Volterra, V., Pace, C., Pennacchi, B., & Corazza, S. (1995). Advanced learning technology for a bilingual education of deaf children. *American Annals of the Deaf, 140*, 402-409.

Web-based Education Commission. (2000, December). *Report to the President and U.S. Congress.* Washington, DC: Author.

Winn, W. (1997). *Learning in hyperspace.* Retrieved March 27, 2004, from http:// www.umuc.edu/ide/potentialWEB97/

John Carey
Carey Dimmitt

The Web and School Counseling

SUMMARY. The Web and related technologies are creating a revolution in the practice of school counseling. This paper describes emerging trends and identifies critical issues that need to be addressed to facilitate increased use. The article summarizes current uses and identifies ways the Web can be used to improve practice and professional competence. To make full use of the potential of Web-based technology, we believe that the school counseling profession needs to (a) develop a research base that identifies best practices in technology use for promoting both effective school counseling practice and professional development education; (b) develop and disseminate standards for ethical and professional technology use in school counseling practices that are based on both professional judgment and research; (c) conduct a national study that describes current uses of Web-based technology, identifies current school counselor competencies, and determines the most important ways technology can enhance professional practice; and (d) develop an extensive Web-based professional development initiative to support stan-

JOHN CAREY is Professor and Director, National Center for School Counseling Outcome Research, University of Massachusetts, Amherst, MA 01003 (E-mail: jcarey@educ.umass.edu).
CAREY DIMMITT is Associate Director, National Center for School Counseling Outcome Research, University of Massachusetts, Amherst, MA 01003 (E-mail: cdimmitt@educ.umass.edu).

[Haworth co-indexing entry note]: "The Web and School Counseling." Carey, John, and Carey Dimmitt. Co-published simultaneously in *Computers in the Schools* (The Haworth Press, Inc.) Vol. 21, No. 3/4, 2004, pp. 69-79; and: *Web-Based Learning in K-12 Classrooms: Opportunities and Challenges* (ed: Jay Blanchard, and James Marshall) The Haworth Press, Inc., 2004, pp. 69-79. Single or multiple copies of this article are available for a fee from The Haworth Document Delivery Service [1-800-HAWORTH, 9:00 a.m. - 5:00 p.m. (EST). E-mail address: docdelivery@haworthpress.com].

dards-based reform efforts in school counseling and to initiate school counselors into e-learning technologies. *[Article copies available for a fee from The Haworth Document Delivery Service: 1-800-HAWORTH. E-mail address: <docdelivery@haworthpress.com> Website: <http://www.HaworthPress.com> © 2004 by The Haworth Press, Inc. All rights reserved.]*

KEYWORDS. School counseling, Internet, professional development, counselor, technology, education, Web-based technology, standards-based

The practice of school counseling is in flux. School counseling programs are transitioning to a standards-based model of practice. In addition, direct student access to career, vocational, college, and self-assessment information via the Internet is requiring the development of new models for academic and career planning. Counselor educators are developing expertise in Web-based approaches to help school counselors acquire and extend their competencies. Professional and ethical standards for the use of technology in school counseling practice are being developed. Successful implementation of conscious, intentional change in all of these areas is an ongoing challenge but ultimately bodes well for school counseling programs.

Currently, the role of school counselors and the nature of school counseling programs are changing in ways that require school counselors to develop different skill sets in order to be effective. School counselors need to become more facile in the use of computer technology that supports student data management, data analysis, data-based planning, program management, program evaluation, and the effective presentation of results. A paradigm shift is necessary as well, with a focus on evidence-based practices and on student achievement as the ultimate outcome measure of school counselor success.

To deal effectively with these changes, extensive professional development and changes in the content of university-based preparation programs are needed. Web-based approaches can have a significant role in promoting the learning necessary for reform.

ACCESS TO INFORMATION
AND SELF-ASSESSMENT INSTRUMENTS

Assuring that all students and their families have the critical information needed to make vocational, career, and educational planning decisions has always been an important part of the school counselor role. In the past few years, an exponential increase in the level of direct access of students and their families to information supporting career, vocational, and educational decision-making has occurred via the World Wide Web (Stevens & Lundberg, 1998). Career and education information is accessible through both government Web sites (e.g., the Department of Labor) and commercial Web sites (e.g., the College Board). Previously, school counselors controlled students' access to information because the information was housed in school resource rooms. Counselors were able to insure the accuracy of information and determine whether it would be helpful. If students have not developed a consistent approach to making decisions, overloading them with additional information may not be helpful and may actually be counterproductive.

Similarly, students and their families have direct access to Web-based self-assessment instruments, some of which are free and some of which charge for personalized reports. Instruments purporting to measure aspects of personality and career interests are now easily available. Documentation of the psychometric soundness of these instruments differs widely. In the past, school counselors regulated access to self-assessment instruments. They were therefore in the position to (a) evaluate assessment devices for psychometric quality, (b) evaluate student issues and concerns to assure that the assessment instrument was appropriate, (c) insure that assessment results were interpreted correctly, and that they were given the proper weight as one component in an overall process of self-understanding.

The genie is out of the bottle and cannot be put back again. The unprecedented increase in direct access by students and their families requires that school counselors develop new approaches to assuring quality and appropriateness of information. School counselors must carefully evaluate the accuracy and quality of information before referring students and their families to a Web-based source. Sabella (1999) has noted that students and their families would consider the inclusion of a link to a career information Web site provided on a school counseling program Web site to be an endorsement of the quality of the linked information. Before referring students to a site, school counselors must consider for whom the site would be helpful. School counseling program links should include descriptive information about the benefits and limitations of the linked site. School counselors need to pay more attention to building students' media literacy skills so that they are better equipped to differentiate between good and bad information. Finally, school counselors need to be available as guides who can provide well-advertised opportunities for students and families to evaluate and personalize Web information. Used effectively, Internet-based resources can be a powerful component of a school-based career development program (Refvem, Plante, & Osborne, 2000).

COUNSELOR STANDARDS AND PRACTICES

In general, counselors have been slow to incorporate instructional technology into their training programs. However, in recent years there have been many changes that should increase school counselors, skills in using Web-based resources and other technology. Counselor training programs (pre-service and in-service) have begun to clarify the technology skills needed for effective counseling.

The 2001 edition of the Council on the Accreditation of Counseling and Related Educational Programs (CACREP) training standards includes several related to technology. CACREP-approved programs must ensure that school counseling students are knowledgeable about:

- Web-based career information and computer-based career information systems.
- Technology-based career development applications and strategies, including computer-assisted career guidance and information systems and appropriate Web sites.
- Computer-managed and computer-assisted student assessment methods.
- Technology and statistical methods used to conduct research and program evaluation.
- Current and emerging technology in education and school counseling to assist students, families, and educators in using resources that promote informed academic, career, and personal/social choices.
- The use of technology in the design, implementation, monitoring and evaluation of a comprehensive school counseling program.

The Technology Interest Network of the Association for Counselor Education and Supervision (ACES Technology Interest Network, 1999; Sandhu, 2001) has developed specific technology competencies for graduates of counselor education programs. At the completion of a counselor education program, students should be able to:

- Use productivity software to develop Web pages, group presentations, letters, and reports.

- Use audiovisual equipment such as video recorders, audio recorders, projection equipment, video conferencing equipment, and playback units.
- Use computerized statistical packages.
- Use computerized testing, diagnostic, and career decision-making programs with clients.
- Use e-mail.
- Help clients search for various types of counseling-related information via the Internet, including information about careers, employment opportunities, educational and training opportunities, financial assistance/scholarships, treatment procedures, and social and personal information.
- Subscribe to, participate in, and sign off counseling-related list-serves.
- Access and use counseling-related CD-ROM databases.
- Understand the legal and ethical codes related to counseling services via the Internet.
- Understand the strengths and weaknesses of counseling services provided via the Internet.
- Use the Internet for finding and using continuing education opportunities in counseling.
- Evaluate the quality of Internet information.

In addition, school counselor educators have developed their own versions of technology competencies for in-service school counselors (Hartman, 1998; Hines, 2002; Sabella, 2000). Initial investigations have been conducted into the use of technology to support school counselor education practices (Hohenshil & Delorenzo, 1999; Myrick & Sabella, 1995; Lund, 2000; Watson, 2003). Crucially, accessible Web-based supports for learning how to use technology have been developed. Noteworthy among these are Russ Sabella's School Counselor.com (http://www.schoolcounselor.com/) and Bob Turba's Cyber-guidance (http://www.cyberguidance.net/), Web sites which provide support for learning about Web-based applications and Internet resources for school counselors.

PROFESSIONAL STANDARDS

Harris-Bowlsbey (2000) has noted the critical importance of ethical and professional standards for practice governing the appropriate use of technology in the field of counseling. In recent years professional associations have made advances in the development of these standards. However, the standards that exist were generated primarily for mental heath practice and commercial career counseling. While the extrapolation of some of the principles of general professional practice to school-based e-counseling is possible, the school counseling profession currently lacks a statement on the use of technology in professional practice.

The National Board for Certified Counselors (NBCC, 1998) and the National Career Development Association (NCDA, 1997) have developed standards for using the Internet to provide counseling services. These standards are primarily designed for using the Internet to provide services for profit to clients in remote locations. In school counseling contexts, counselors are more likely to interact personally with students and to use the Internet to support rather than supplant face-to-face interaction. NBCC and NCDA standards relevant to school counseling practice include the need to

1. Be able to ensure that the Web-based service is appropriate for a given student.
2. Provide access to periodic face-to-face counseling for Internet service users.
3. Safeguard student confidentiality in Web-based communications through encryption.
4. Ensure that Web-based services are available to students with disabilities.
5. Disclose the nature of client information that is electronically stored, including the length of time that data will be maintained before being destroyed.
6. Assure that Web sites to which the school counseling program links observe ethical and professional practices.

While these general standards are helpful, specific standards for using technology in school counseling are needed. Ideally, these standards would be based upon both professional judgment and research. While initial investigations have been conducted into using technology to support school counseling interventions (D'Andrea, 1995; Stone & Turba, 1999) and school counselor education practices (Hohenshil & Delorenzo, 1999; Myrick & Sabella, 1995; Lund, 2000; Watson, 2003), a research base evaluating the effectiveness of different technology-supported approaches has not yet been developed.

CURRENT PRACTICES

A national survey of school counselor technology use is sorely needed. An action research study of school counselor technology use suggested that school counselors are currently actively experimenting with how Web-based technology can be used to support their work in public schools (Creamer, 2002). They are using Web sites and e-mail to make students and parents aware of services and programs and to support communication with parents (Van Horn & Myrick, 2001). D'Andrea (1995) suggested that school counselors should use the Internet as a source of enriched content in curriculum-based psycho-educational interventions. The extent to which school counselors are actually incorporating Internet resources into guidance lessons is unknown.

Many school counseling program Web sites refer students and parents to other Web sites that contain career and educational information (Van Horn & Myrick, 2001). Some Web sites refer students to free self-assessment inventories. The authors have reviewed a large number of K-12 school counseling program Web sites and have only rarely found information that would help students or their parents evaluate the quality of information contained in the linked external sites. In addition, the authors have found numerous instances of school counseling program Web sites containing links to Web-based self-assessments that have psychometric properties that are unknown or questionable. Unfortunately, many sites are not designed for access by people with disabilities.

Although many school counselors provide short-term crisis counseling and ongoing counseling support to students, judging from the absence of professional reports it does not appear that the use of "cyber counseling" is a common school counseling practice.

COUNSELORS AS CONSUMERS

School counselors, like most professionals, need access to lifelong learning resources to update competencies and develop skills. The American School Counseling Association (http://www.schoolcounselor.org/) Web site contains valuable professional development information and resources on a wide range of topics related to school counselors' work. To use this and other Web-based resources, school counselors must have access to appropriate technologies–and the skills to use them.

Unfortunately, a systematic assessment of the technologies and skills needed by school counselors is missing.

Currently, there is one online professional journal dedicated to counseling and technology issues. In its first five years, the *Journal of Technology in Counseling* (http://jtc.colstate.edu/) has published several useful articles related to school counseling including how to use technology in student advocacy (Stone & Turba, 1999), standards for school counselor technology competence (Hines, 2002), and how to use technology to increase collaboration between school counselors and special educators (Gillam, Hendricks, George, & Baltimore, 2003).

The Educational Resource and Information Center (ERIC) served as an important general source for information on comprehensive school counseling and career development practices. ERIC is currently in transition and its future role is uncertain. The Center for School Counseling Outcome Research maintains a Web site (http://www.umass.edu/schoolcounseling/) that disseminates research monographs related to evidence-based school counseling practices. The center also distributes quarterly research briefs by means of an 11,000 member listserv.

Increasingly, lesson plans relating to school counseling curriculum objectives are available on the Web. Typically these lesson plans have been developed by school counselors and are accessible on school district Web sites. In a much more ambitious effort, Canada's Blueprint for Life Web site (http://206.191.51.163/blueprint/home.cfm) presents a national K-adult curriculum for life-long career development, with learning activities that are keyed to specific student learning objectives. Through this site, school counselors have access to a comprehensive, organized system for planning, delivering, and evaluating developmental, curriculum-based programs that build student competencies in personal management, learning and work exploration, and, life/work building. The Blueprint for Life site is an outstanding demonstration of the use of a Web site to simultaneously make educational resources accessible to users and to organize those resources in order to promote the development and implementation of comprehensive, developmental educational programs.

School counselors often have limited opportunities to access supervision focused on their own competence development. It has been suggested that school counselors can use e-learning technology to consult with remote supervisors and colleagues about problematic cases (Van Horn & Myrick, 2001). Myrick and Sabella (1995) have described how e-mail, Web-based bulletin boards, and instant messaging can be used to support remote supervision and peer consultation, and have suggested ways that these supports can be incorporated in a public school-based program.

Increasingly, counselor education programs are using distance education delivery systems for school counseling courses. It is not clear to what extent these courses are a potential e-learning professional development resource. As noted previously, the school counseling profession is in transition to a standards-based model of practice. This transition has created a need for training in standards-based education practice and data use. Apparently this need is being addressed through live conferences rather than through online delivery mechanisms.

CONCLUSION AND RECOMMENDATIONS

Pre-service and in-service school counselors need to develop new skills to meet the advances in technology that are beginning to impact the efficiency and effectiveness of counseling practices. Since it is clear that e-counseling technologies–and the skills to use them–will have an impact, we recommend the following:

First, the school counseling profession needs a research base that identifies best practices in technology use for promoting both effective school counseling practice and professional development education. At present, most professional articles are focused on demonstrating the potential value of technology use without actually evaluating its efficiency or effectiveness. Ultimately, in order to justify resource allocation, it is important to demonstrate the impact of school counselors' use of Web-based technology on student development.

Second, the school counseling profession needs to develop and disseminate standards for ethical and professional technology use in school counseling practices that are based on both professional judgment and research. The general NBCC and NCDA standards do not adequately address issues endemic to school-based practice. Our cursory review of school counseling program Web sites suggests that many school counselors are unaware of these general professional standards. The American School Counseling Association has developed over 30 position papers on many areas of practice (e.g., character education, multicultural education, and high-stakes testing) but lacks such a statement on effective technology use.

Third, the school counseling profession needs a national study to describe current uses of Web-based technology, identify current school counselor competencies, and determine the most important ways technology can enhance professional practice.

Fourth, the school counseling profession needs to develop an extensive Web-based professional development initiative to support standards-based reform efforts in school counseling and to initiate school counselors into e-learning technologies. The American School Counseling Association ought to foster the development of an integrated e-learning approach to training in ASCA National Model implementation and in the related required quantitative skills. Continuing the profession's practices of disseminating innovative information though live conferences is inefficient and misses an important opportunity to learn how to use a tool for a task for which it is ideally suited.

The school counseling profession has made significant progress in (a) exploring potential uses of technology to enhance services to student and families, (b) identifying critical school counselor competencies, and (c) establishing projects that use e-learning technology to build knowledge and skills. There is an excellent national model for practice and a national community of school counselors who are in the midst of transition and transformation. Now is the time for the profession to ensure that school counselors learn to use e-learning tools for the ultimate benefit of students and their families.

REFERENCES

American School Counselors Association. (2003). *National model for school counseling programs*. Alexandria, VA: American School Counselors Association.

Association for Counselor Education and Supervision Technology Interest Network. (1999). *Technical competencies for counselor education students: Recommended guidelines for program development*. Retrieved from http://www.acesonline.net/oldcomps.htm

Creamer, M. (2002). Technology utilization in the field of school counseling: An action research study. *Action Research Exchange, 1*. Retrieved from http://chiron.valdosta.edu/are/

D'Andrea, M. (1995). Using computer technology to promote multicultural awareness among elementary school-age students. *Elementary School Guidance and Counseling, 30*, 45-54.

Gillam, S., Hendricks, M., George, J., & Baltimore, M. (2003). The utilization of technology to assist collaboration efforts among school counselors and special educators with the implementation of IDEA 97. *Journal of Technology in Counseling, 3*. Retrieved from http://jtc.colstate.edu/vol3_1/Gillam/Gillam.htm

Harris-Bowlsbey, J. (2000). The Internet: Blessing or bane for the counseling profession? In J. Bloom & G. Walz (Eds.), *Cybercounseling and cyberlearning: Strategies and resources for the millennium* (pp. 39-49). Alexandria, VA: American Counseling Association.

Hartman, K. (1998). Technology and the school counselor. *Education Week, 18*. Retrieved from http://www.edweek.org

Hines, P. (2002). Student technology competencies for school counseling programs. *Journal of Technology in Counseling, 2*. Retrieved from http://jtc.colstate.edu/vol2_2/hines/hines.htm

Hohenshil, T., & Delorenzo, D. (1999). Teaching career development via the Internet. *Career Planning and Adult Development Journal, 19*, 53-60.

Lund, D. (2000). Integrating on-line technology into counseling curriculum: Emerging humanistic factors. *Journal of Humanistic Counseling, Education and Development, 38*, 142-151.

Myrick, R., & Sabella, R. (1995). Cyberspace: A new place for counselor supervision. *Elementary School Guidance and Counseling, 30*, 35-44.

National Board for Certified Counselors. (1998). *Standards for the ethical practice of Web counseling*. Greensboro, NC: Author.

National Career Development Association. (1997). *Guidelines for the use of the Internet for provision of career information and planning services*. Columbus, OH: Author.

Refvem, J., Plante, J., & Osborne, W. (2000). Interactive career counseling in middle and secondary schools: Integrating the use of the Internet into school career development programs. In J. Bloom & G. Walz (Eds.), *Cybercounseling and cyberlearning: Strategies and resources for the millennium* (pp. 115-127). Alexandria, VA: American Counseling Association.

Sabella, R. (2000). School counseling and technology. In J. Wittmer (Ed.), *Managing your school counseling program: K-12 development strategies* (2nd ed.). Minneapolis, MN: Educational Media Corporation.

Sabella, R. (1999). *SchoolCounselor.com: A friendly and practical guide to the World Wide WEB*. Minneapolis, MN: Educational Media Corporation.

Sandhu, D. (2001). *Elementary school counseling in the new millennium*. Alexandria, VA: American Counseling Association.

Stevens, D., & Lundberg, D. (1998). The emergence of the Internet: Enhancing career counseling. *Journal of Career Development, 24*, 195-208.

Stone, C., & Turba, R. (1999). School counselors using technology for advocacy. *Journal of Technology, 1*. Retrieved from http://jtc.colstate.edu/vol1_1/advocacy.htm

Van Horn, S., & Myrick, R. (2001). Computer technology and the 21st century counselor. *Professional School Counseling, 5*, 124-130.

Watson, J. (2003). Computer-based supervision: Implementing computer technology into the delivery of counseling supervision. *Journal of Technology in Counseling, 3*. Retrieved from http://jtc.colstate.edu/vol3_1/Watson/Watson.htm

Lynne Schrum

The Web and Virtual Schools

SUMMARY. This paper focuses on the role of government in the growth of Web-based virtual schools. First, it describes the current evolving situation. It then discusses ways in which U.S. federal, state, and local governments have developed virtual schools, and presents some information about international initiatives in this area. It also identifies similarities and differences among virtual schools. Finally, challenges for Web-based virtual schools are discussed. *[Article copies available for a fee from The Haworth Document Delivery Service: 1-800-HAWORTH. E-mail address: <docdelivery@haworthpress.com> Website: <http://www.HaworthPress.com> © 2004 by The Haworth Press, Inc. All rights reserved.]*

KEYWORDS. Virtual schools, technology-enhanced learning, online learning, charter schools, state education, computers and education, home schooling, ICT, distance learning

OVERVIEW

Interest in e-learning and virtual schools has grown enormously since its public emergence in the late 1980s, especially in the United States

LYNNE SCHRUM is Professor and Chair, Department of Teaching and Learning, University of Utah, Salt Lake City, UT 84112 (E-mail: Lynne.Schrum@ed.utah.edu).

[Haworth co-indexing entry note]: "The Web and Virtual Schools." Schrum, Lynne. Co-published simultaneously in *Computers in the Schools* (The Haworth Press, Inc.) Vol. 21, No. 3/4, 2004, pp. 81-89; and: *Web-Based Learning in K-12 Classrooms: Opportunities and Challenges* (ed: Jay Blanchard, and James Marshall) The Haworth Press, Inc., 2004, pp. 81-89. Single or multiple copies of this article are available for a fee from The Haworth Document Delivery Service [1-800-HAWORTH, 9:00 a.m. - 5:00 p.m. (EST). E-mail address: docdelivery@haworthpress.com].

(*Education Week*, 2002). Today, many states and countries offer virtual schools. Its earlier parent, distance education, has been around since a reliable postal service, and has long been viewed as a way to offer learning to those who are geographically or philosophically separated from traditional schools. Distance education has also been viewed as an alternative to traditional schools by those who have obligations that limit their ability to attend classes, or perhaps prefer to learn in non-classroom-based ways.

But, just exactly what is *e-learning*? Its definition seems to vary widely throughout the world. For the purposes of this paper, e-learning means the teaching of formal, credit-bearing classes through Web-based computer resources, minimally including hyperlinks and/or the Internet, and synchronous and/or asynchronous communication (Kinash, 2002). E-learning, or synonymously Web-based or online learning, can be used alongside and in tandem with traditional learning. When this combination occurs, it has been termed *blended learning*.

The growth of virtual schools has been rapid and widespread. Originally labeled "virtual high schools," they are now focused on the entire K-12 spectrum; however, most classes or courses are still geared toward upper-level students (Clark, 2001). In a comprehensive study of virtual schools, the Peak Report (2002) found that approximately 200,000 students were expected to enroll in an online course in one of the 88 programs in the United States during the school year 2002-2003. The most commonly reported cost for each course was $300, although the costs varied widely. Calculus was the online advanced placement (AP) course offered most by schools (Clark, 2001, p. i).

A difference exists between "complete" virtual school programs (degree granting) and programs where students simply take courses online. Regardless of the difference, all virtual school programs reach learners who may have been unable or unwilling to gain access through traditional means. Reasons for this may include illness, disability, learning challenges, geographic location (rural communities, for example), or other personal circumstances, such as additions to a home schooling plan. Regardless of the differences, all programs share common challenges. To help educators, parents, teachers, and policymakers meet these challenges, state, federal, and nongovernmental organizations have begun to act. For example, the Wisconsin Department of Education has created a *Policy and Informational Advisory* on virtual schools (http://www.dpi.state.wi.us). This document offers a discussion of important issues related to virtual education and is the first step toward the development of uniform standards and expectations.

U.S. FEDERAL INITIATIVES

For many years the U.S. government has been interested in expanding student access to virtual schools and expanding the dissemination of information about these schools. Most initiatives have focused on science, medicine, and agriculture education. While these initiatives were not specifically related to K-12 education, they often have positive side effects. For example, the American Memory Project (http://memory.loc.gov/) makes the vast collection of rare and primary documents and files of the Library of Congress accessible and useful online for classrooms and teachers. Another useful initiative is the Distance Learning Resource Network (www.dlrn.org) which compiles online resources for teaching with technology.

There are a few initiatives specifically focused on K-12 virtual schools, however. One well known is the Virtual High School (VHS). VHS evolved out of the Concord Consortium, which was originally funded by a U.S. Department of Education Technology Innovation Grant. The model for VHS is that of a collaborative between schools. A unique aspect of this project is that schools commit to participate and then local educators take an online course to learn how to design and teach online. These local educators design and offer courses, and their participation allows their local students to participate in other educators' online classes. Early research on VHS (Roblyer & Elbaum, 1999/2000) demonstrated that its potential was great; however, implementation would be improved with better preparation for both teaching and learning in this environment.

After the initial federal funding, the Concord Consortium turned VHS into a self-sustaining, nonprofit educational institution. It is now supported by student fees and grants to promote and study the effects of this program. Currently, VHS offers grants for advanced placement (AP) classes to low-wealth schools in an effort to bring AP and pre-AP classes to middle and high school students who otherwise lack access.

U.S. STATE AND LOCAL INITIATIVES

State Schools

Although the U.S. government may have played a role in supporting virtual schools, state-sanctioned schools are the most common. Recent calculations (April 2004) suggest that 32 states have some kind of

Web-based schooling programs: 12 have virtual schools and five more are in the planning stages for virtual schools. Many of these schools offer learning experiences to students beyond their state borders. For example, the Utah Electronic High School (http://ehs.uen.org/?bbatt=Y) offers courses free to any Utah student and charges others (available to students around the world) a modest fee. An alternative model is that of the Kentucky Virtual High School (http://www.kvhs.org/), which only offers courses to students in Kentucky.

Some states have moved to a different type of state-supported virtual school, in which the K-12 entity is sponsored by state-funded universities. The University of Nebraska-Lincoln Independent Study High School (http://dcs.unl.edu/ishs/) offers two curricula and diplomas (college preparatory and general education). The courses are offered to students throughout the world, including international students, and everyone pays approximately the same cost (no advantage to in-state students).

Perhaps the most well-known example of this type of Web-based e-learning is the Florida Virtual School (FLVS) (http://www.flvs.net/). This statewide, Web-based public high school offers structured curriculum online. The Florida legislature initially funded the FLVS as a pilot project in 1997, at $1.3 million to begin course development with a limited student enrollment. In 2000 the Florida legislature established FLVS as an independent education entity with a separate governing board appointed by the governor. As the largest of the state-run Web-based e-learning options, FLVS offers courses to students on a one-course basis or as an entire curriculum.

Another well-known program is the Arkansas Virtual High School (http://arkansashigh.k12.ar.us/avhsmain.htm), a pilot project funded by the Arkansas Department of Education. Its purpose is to "provide an online alternative learning environment for the students of Arkansas' public schools who need assistance in completing coursework that is difficult to receive due to factors such as schedule conflicts, homebound due to extenuating circumstances, and other factors that might impede a student's progress through grades 9-12" (Arkansas Virtual High School, np). This Arkansas school, limited to Arkansas students, is completely free of charge. Students are required to register through their local schools and the courses are transferred to their regular high school transcripts and apply toward graduation.

The Michigan Virtual High School (MVHS) (http://www.mivhs. org/) is another state-funded program but with a different twist. MVHS offers online exam preparation for tests like the SAT, PSAT, MEAP, and College Board exams. In addition, MVHS offers online assessment and multimedia tools to teachers and provides online certification classes for teachers.

State Charter Schools

A recent and growing trend is the creation of state-funded charter virtual schools. These may be part of public school districts or they may be separate nonprofit or for-profit organizations. These schools must operate under charter school legislation but do use state funds to support their staff and to provide technology to families and students. These schools serve home-schooled students and students needing alternative educational opportunities. At last estimate, these schools enrolled about 21,000 students in 16 states, according to the Center for Education Reform (http://www.edreform.com/). One example of these schools is the Basehor-Linwood Virtual Charter School in Kansas (Clark, 2001). This school provides public education for K-12 home-schooled students across the state with a full diploma program and includes a district-certified teacher for each elementary grade and for each secondary content area.

District Schools

Government-supported e-learning schools have also been sponsored by local school districts. For example, in Eugene, Oregon, Cyberschool was originally designed to teach Eugene's students about the vast resources online. However, it quickly evolved into full courses, many not available locally, and is now serving a global population of learners and teachers.

INTERNATIONAL INITIATIVES

Web-based e-learning has become important throughout the world so much so that in 2002, UNESCO reported that the impact of e-learning is "already significant in all developed countries, and the great majority of developing countries are, despite difficulties and fears, seeking to take part in the emerging global educational community" (p. 12). UNESCO is not alone. The European Union (EU) has also encouraged virtual school initiatives in several of its member countries through a collaborative organization called European Schoolnet (www.eun.org/). Much of Schoolnet's efforts are focused on *virtual learning environments* (VLE), which is an umbrella term that encompasses a variety of activities dedicated to changing the nature of what happens in a traditional class and also includes completely virtual environments. According to a recent report (European Schoolnet, 2003),

> Ten out of 17 national agencies fund the development and localisation of VLEs at the national level, and about 60% of them have a high priority for VLEs in their national policies. About two thirds of respondent schools use an in-house or open source VLE, whereas commercial products represent about one third of the VLEs in the field. (p. 5)

For example, Denmark has begun its Virtual Gymnasium for upper secondary education (European Schoolnet, 2003). Europe is only one of many regions in which virtual schools are gaining interest and support from governmental organizations. In Israel, Canada, Australia, and the United Kingdom there are government-supported virtual schools. In each of these countries the programs vary as to their goals and purpose, as well as the intended audience.

CHALLENGES

Statewide and local schools share some common challenges (Clark, 2000). Virtual school efforts have a potential to permanently and dramatically change the nature of K-12 schools and, not surprisingly, the traditional school community is struggling to understand and respond. Several years ago, Rutkowski (1999) reported that "school boards, school districts, and national and state educational agencies will likely be compelled to modify many of their requirements and create new standards of teaching and learning" (p. 75). Rutkowski's remarks remain true today. Virtual schools offer solutions to many of education's oldest challenges. But in doing so, they raise a new set of challenges.

Challenge 1. Perhaps the most significant challenge is the need to ensure digital equity. Overall, it is important for those contemplating offering Web-based learning to remember the reality of learners' individual needs. Access is important, especially when public money is used to fund and support these educational institutions, and must also include those learners who have physical challenges, thus requiring the use of universal design. Universally designed objects are useable by almost everyone without special modification, adaptation, or use of assistive devices, so that "universally designed computer interfaces are user-friendly for most, regardless of technical proficiency, sensory impairment and/or personality and learning styles and preferences" (Kinash, 2002, p. 4). In addition, classes focused only on advanced courses ultimately leave out students who are at risk for not completing their K-12 studies (Hurley, 2002). Another digital equity challenge is funding. Many of the virtual school opportunities are currently funded by governmental money and yet the costs for taking each course may be significant to the learners who pay for them. Each organization seems to have different regulations for course payment (e.g., when a student is ill and unable to attend a traditional class), but students with resources certainly are better able to take e-learning courses, and are more likely to have regular access to computer equipment at home.

Challenge 2. Issues that have always plagued traditional distance education are also relevant to e-learning schools. These include teacher certification (Do educators need to be certified in the state in which the institution is funded and created?), the availability of credit at a student's home school, and the challenge of obtaining something as simple as a transcript (Schrum, 2002).

Oblender (2002) reported on a school that offered virtual courses for many years and yet had a consistent dropout rate of almost 25%. Consequently, this school designed a hybrid course model so that students had a set time to meet with a teacher in a computer lab. By also setting aside a specific time and place to do their work, students reported less chance of becoming lost, ignoring the subject, or falling behind, and the dropout rate fell to less than 2%. Unfortunately, while this may be helpful to students who attend a traditional high school, it is not helpful to those who take e-learning courses from home.

Challenge 3. Quality control is an issue in all educational communities, especially in today's climate of data-driven decision-making (Center on Education Policy, 2002). In e-learning situations it is even more significant and perhaps requires additional attention to ongoing evaluation. As mentioned, while Roblyer and Elbaum (1999-2000) reported some positive results for some online courses, the literature is limited. State legislators are going to expect results that go beyond the currently available information, and more importantly, parents, educators, and the community are going to expect information on learning outcomes. The National Education Association (NEA) recently released a document focused on examining and assessing the quality of online high school classes (2002). They specifically recognized the need for these courses to "address the unique social, educational, and emotional needs of high school students" (np).

REFERENCES

Andrews, K., & Marshall, K. (2000). Making learning connections through telelearning. *Educational Leadership*, *58*(2), 53-56.

Arkansas Virtual High School. (2004). Home Page. Retrieved August 2003 from http://arkansashigh.k12.ar.us/avhs_main.htm

Center on Education Policy. (2002). *Preserving principles of public education in an online world: What policymakers should be asking about virtual schools.* Washington, DC: Author.

Clark, T. (2000). *Virtual high schools: State of the states.* Macomb, IL: Center for the Application of Information Technologies.

Clark, T. (2001). *Virtual schools: Trends and issues.* San Francisco: WestEd and Distance Learning Resource Network.

Education Week (2002, May 9). *E-defining education: How virtual schools and online instruction are transforming teaching and learning.* Themed Issue. Bethesda, MD: Author.

European SchoolNet. (2003) *Virtual learning environments for European schools: A survey and commentary.* Retrieved October 2003 from http://www.ictliteracy.info/resources/VLE_restricted_2003.pdf

Hurley, R. (2002). Fine-tuning an online high school to benefit at-risk students. *T. H. E. Journal*, *30*(4), 33-34, 36, 38, 40.

Kinash, S. (2002). *Online learning in American and Canadian post-secondary institutions.* Calgary: University of Calgary. Retrieved September 2003 from http://www.crds.org/contacts/faculty_pages/kinash/resources/reportone.pdf

Mittelman, T. (2001). The establishment of a virtual high school in Israel. *Educational Technology Research and Development*, *49*(1), 84-93.

National Education Association. (2002). *Guide to online high school courses.* Washington, DC: Author. Retrieved September 2003 from http://www.nea.org/technology/onlinecourseguide.html

Oblender, T. (2002). A hybrid course model: One solution to the high online drop-out rate. *Learning and Leading with Technology*, *29*(6), 42-46.

Peak Group. (2002). *Virtual schools across America: Trends in K-12 online education 2002.* Los Altos, CA: Author.

Roblyer, M., & Elbaum, B. (1999/2000). Virtual learning? Research on virtual high schools. *Learning and Leading with Technology*, *27*(4), 58-61.

Roblyer, M., & Marshall, J. (2002/2003). Predicting success of virtual high school students: Preliminary results from an educational success prediction instrument. *Journal of Research on Technology in Education*, *35*(2), 241-255.

Rutkowski, K. (1999). Virtual schools: Charting new frontiers. *MultiMedia, 6*(1), 74-79.

Schrum, L. (1998). Online education in the information age: A study of emerging pedagogy. In B. Cahoon (Ed.), *Adult learning and the Internet* (pp. 53-61). San Francisco: Jossey-Bass.

Schrum, L. (2002). Oh what wonders you will see: Distance education past, present and future. *Learning and Leading with Technology, 30*(3), 6-9, 20-21.

UNESCO. (2002). *Open and distance learning: Trends, policy and strategic considerations.* Retrieved December 2003 from http://unesdoc.unesco.org/images/0012/001284/128463e.pdf

Wisconsin Department of Education. (nd). *Policy and informational advisory.* Retrieved September 2003 from http://www.dpi.state.wi.us

Michael Milone

Exemplary Web-Based Schools

SUMMARY. Exemplary Web-based schools are as different as they are similar. The schools featured in this section have applied technology in unique ways to meet the needs of their students. Five examples are cited across the U.S.: Lemon Grove School District, Lemon Grove, California; Virginia Beach City Public Schools, Virginia Beach, Virginia; Carlsbad Unified School District, Carlsbad, California; Monsignor Bonner High School, Drexel Hill, Pennsylvania; South Burlington High School, South Burlington, Vermont; and Canutillo Elementary School, Canutillo, Texas. *[Article copies available for a fee from The Haworth Document Delivery Service: 1-800-HAWORTH. E-mail address: <docdelivery@haworthpress.com> Website: <http://www.HaworthPress.com> © 2004 by The Haworth Press, Inc. All rights reserved.]*

KEYWORDS. Technology, computers, schools, education, exemplary, model, Web-based, learning, excellence, classroom

Although it is not easy to define what an exemplary technology program is, recognizing one when you see it is pretty obvious. Moreover, while exemplary programs are notable for their distinctiveness, they share some common characteristics.

MICHAEL MILONE is Field Editor, *Technology and Learning Magazine*, Placitas, NM 87043 (E-mail: mmilone@aol.com).

[Haworth co-indexing entry note]: "Exemplary Web-Based Schools." Milone, Michael. Co-published simultaneously in *Computers in the Schools* (The Haworth Press, Inc.) Vol. 21, No. 3/4, 2004, pp. 91-99; and: *Web-Based Learning in K-12 Classrooms: Opportunities and Challenges* (ed: Jay Blanchard, and James Marshall) The Haworth Press, Inc., 2004, pp. 91-99. Single or multiple copies of this article are available for a fee from The Haworth Document Delivery Service [1-800-HAWORTH, 9:00 a.m. - 5:00 p.m. (EST). E-mail address: docdelivery@haworthpress.com].

Exemplary technology programs are often defined by one of two characteristics. In some cases, they reflect a tradition of excellence that has been in place for years. In other cases, exemplary programs are the result of the dedication of a single "champion" or small group of educators. Over time, these technology enthusiasts draw the rest of the school community into their circle. In all cases, exemplary programs use technology in general, and the Internet in particular, as a tool to accomplish various goals. These goals are setting-specific and are defined by the needs of students, teachers, parents, and the community as a whole. Surprisingly, increasing achievement as measured by traditional means is rarely one of the goals, but it is often achieved as an ancillary outcome.

The programs cited in this paper are just a few of the outstanding technology programs in U.S. schools. There are hundreds of programs that are just as remarkable across the globe, and all of the educators who are involved with them deserve recognition for the opportunities and encouragement they are providing to K-12 students today.

EXEMPLARY SCHOOLS

Lemon Grove School District
Lemon Grove, California

In the early 1990s, Lemon Grove School District did something remarkable. It created a wireless network to connect the district's schools with one another. This intranet was one of the first of its kind in the nation, but the district was still not satisfied. In a remarkable move, it partnered with the local cable company, Cox Communications, to offer a high-speed connection between the schools and students' homes. Project LemonLINK was born (www.lgsd.k12.ca.us/lgsd/default.htm).

Darryl LaGace, the district's director of information systems, wanted to develop a network in which the district would serve as the center of a learning community. A microwave tower located at the district office connects each school and city facility to the network. Fiber-optic links supplement the wireless intranet. All city government facilities are part of the system, including city hall, the fire department, public works, the recreation department, the community center, the youth center, and the senior center. Every classroom is also connected to the network, which gives teachers and students high-speed access to the Internet.

Lemon Grove is a suburb of San Diego, California, that was once a rural community. Many of the students and their families would not be able to afford a computer or access to high-speed Internet service. Through a unique school/community/business collaboration, the cost of Internet service through the local cable system has been reduced significantly, and supplemental funding is available to families that cannot afford even this reduced cost.

Using thin-client network equipment, students and families can now access online educational resources from home 24 hours a day. This access gives students an opportunity to complete homework assignments online and submit them through e-mail. Parents can communicate with teachers through the network, and families can take advantage of educational resources such as current and archived periodicals, newspapers, and Encarta Online Deluxe, thus extending literacy beyond the traditional classroom.

As is the case with many districts, Lemon Grove recognized that inadequate access to technology may inhibit the academic progress of many students. Under the guidance of project director Barbara Allen, the initial goal of LemonLINK was to provide one computer with Internet connectivity for every four students. Even though this ratio is admirable, it was simply not good enough if students were to receive the kind of interactive learning that Lemon Grove educators envisioned. To increase access to a 1:2 computer-to-student ratio, the network appliances developed for the home connection were installed in district classrooms by replacing half the classroom allocation of CPUs with three times as many network appliances.

The flood of technology that is available in Lemon Grove, in conjunction with an aggressive staff development program and high academic expectations, has had a meaningful impact on learning. A number of years ago, seven of the district's eight schools were identified as underperforming, with test scores far below the state average. In 2001, however, three of Lemon Grove's schools achieved the largest improvement in test scores in San Diego County. A year later, three other schools in the district were recognized by the California Department of Education as Title I High Performing Schools. Just last year, a district middle school was highlighted as one of the top ten middle schools in the country.

Virginia Beach City Public Schools
Virginia Beach, Virginia

Not many districts publish a hard-bound book containing articles written by district educators, but that's exactly what Virginia Beach

City Public Schools (VBCPS) has done. *Tapestry of Knowledge*, Volume III, is a collection of perspectives about the best uses of technology in the Beach's schools and is a tribute to both the district's educators and its commitment to using technology to optimize the educational experiences for all students (www.vbschools.com/tapestry).

The rise of VBCPS as an exemplary technology district can be attributed in great part to its superintendent, Dr. Timothy Jenney. In the eight years he's been at the helm, he's turned the district from a technology backwater into a model of best practices. The transformation has not been without controversy, and many locals have had a difficult time adjusting to his leadership style. Nonetheless, the results speak for themselves.

The flagship of the district's technology initiative is the Advanced Technology Center. The ATC is a joint venture of the city of Virginia Beach, Tidewater Community College, and Virginia Beach City Public Schools. It's an educational and training facility that serves the needs of the district's students, graduates, and businesses. Costing more than $22 million, the facility is one of the most sophisticated workforce/technology projects in the United States.

The ATC offers students and the community the latest in technology-based curricula as well as distance learning and teleconference facilities, a technology theater, and computer labs. The center also includes a manufacturing lab, quality assurance software, a high-quality lathe system, tabletop training consoles, computer integrated management workstations, and industrial process control software.

Every school in the district has a dedicated computer lab and a resource specialist whose function is to assist teachers in incorporating technology into core courses. These specialists help teachers use innovative strategies such as WebQuests to increase student motivation and vary the learning experience. In addition to local technology, 23 distance learning classes are now offered through the Internet. These classes typically involve advanced learning in subject areas that require teachers with special backgrounds, such as discrete mathematics.

The district's budget supports a five-year replacement cycle to ensure that students are working with the latest technology. In one school, Landstown High School, a "school-within-a-school" has been developed. The Technology Academy provides an enriched environment for students who have the talent and interest to push technology to the next level.

Recognizing that people are at the heart of any significant change in education, the district initiated a five-year plan to encourage staff to acquire basic technology competencies. A stipend of $300 was offered to those who could demonstrate mastery without district training. This novel approach saved the district money and helped develop a spirit of self-determination among staff. Superintendent Jenney led the staff-development initiative by example and is completing an executive MBA degree.

Like many other districts, VBCPS understands that its relationship with the community is as important as what it does internally. As part of its public relations effort, the district created a Web site (vbschools. com) that receives upwards of a million hits a month. The Web site was featured in the April 2002 issue of *Ladies Home Journal.*

As you might expect, distance learning is part of the district's technology offerings. It is available in all 11 high schools in the district as well as a number of middle schools. Eventually, all the middle schools will be able to participate.

Even the most trivial of considerations has been affected by the district's technology initiative. Much of the paper that inundates a typical district has been digitized and stored in an electronic database. In addition, many of the public records like school board minutes are available online through the Internet.

Carlsbad Unified School District
Carlsbad, California

While the competitors in the San Diego Triathlon Challenge, a fundraiser for the Challenged Athletes Foundation, prepared for their event, local print and broadcast media circulated among them, gathering information for their reports later in the day. One group of journalists represented an award-winning news organization from an unlikely source, Carlsbad High School.

Carlsbad High School TV (CHSTV) was founded by Douglas Green, a teacher of broadcast journalism. The project began in the 1990s as a middle-school news program, the "Viking View Show." The 45-minute news magazine was produced each semester, and it soon attracted national attention. In 1996, one of its features was included in the CNN Student Video Journalism Awards, the only middle school asked to participate.

Several years ago, Green was asked to move his journalism class to Carlsbad High School. Many of his students had worked with him in middle school, so the transition was seamless. Today, CHSTV is the only live daily student broadcast on the Internet (chstv.com). In addition to school news, student journalists cover local and national events, simulcasting their reports on the Internet and the local cable channel.

What's remarkable about Green's program is that it's still a low-cost operation. Although the program was started with $2,000 from the district, it receives an average of about $500 a year now. The bulk of its funding comes from foundations and other outside sources.

In 2003, CHSTV received two National Student Television Awards for Excellence from the National Television Academy, the organization that sponsors the Emmy awards. In fact, 2003 marked the first year that CHSTV was eligible to compete because in prior years only colleges and universities were eligible.

The equipment used by the Carlsbad students is broadcast quality digital video. Although the broadcast appears to originate from a dedicated studio, the set is actually a classroom. The background is virtual so that student news anchors appear to be sitting in a professional studio.

Students in Green's program receive a well-rounded education, becoming familiar with all aspects of broadcasting. At the center of the program is communicating through writing and speaking. Students learn how to write a balanced story that reflects various points of view and how to deliver the message in a way that appeals to an audience. They certainly learn about technology, but as a tool for delivering their message, not for its own sake.

Monsignor Bonner High School
Drexel Hill, Pennsylvania

Technically, GradeConnect.com doesn't fit with the rest of the programs featured in this section, but it certainly is exemplary. Louis Osinski, a teacher at Monsignor Bonner High School in Drexel Hill, Pennsylvania, created a free Web site for teachers, who can use it to post grades, homework assignments, announcements, and links to other Web sites. They can also generate progress reports and use the site to send e-mail to students and parents.

The genesis of GradeConnect.com, like so many other developments, was necessity. The teachers at Bonner had been using a popular online grade book system, and the company that offered it decided to start charging for the program. The school simply didn't have the thousands of dollars it would cost to license the program, so Osinski decided to develop a comparable program and tailor it for secondary schools. As the co-owner of Media Web Site Design, Osinski found that the task was certainly within his capabilities, and with almost daily input from fellow teachers, the site quickly evolved into much more than just a method for calculating grades. It became a communication tool among teachers, students, and parents.

After a period of beta testing, GradeConnect.com was launched in September of 2003, and currently there are 3,600 users among 15 schools, including one site in Hong Kong. The costs of the site are paid for both by donations and sponsored advertisements. A school has the option of opting out of any advertisements for a fee that would replace the advertisement income.

South Burlington High School
South Burlington, Vermont

The Imaging Lab at South Burlington High School (imagelab. sbschools.net/) is arguably one of the most advanced technology installations in the country. The lab began in the 1990s with some equipment that was pretty low-tech, even for the time. Tim Comolli, the lab's director, thought his students were doing some exciting stuff, so he invited the president of a local video production house to drop by. The visitor thought the students had the potential to do much more, so he donated a $5,000 computer to the program. The lab took off, and thanks to continuing donations and the support of everyone involved, has grown into a world-class facility.

The American School Board Journal featured the lab a few years ago, and Comolli has been recognized with several awards, including one from the National Education Association (NEA), Foundation for the Improvement of Education. The Imaging Lab is so popular that there's a waiting list to join, and both Comolli and his students offer courses for art teachers from other schools within the district, as well as from other districts, and they offer evening classes for adults from the community.

While students in most schools use the Internet as a resource, at South Burlington, it's a career move. The school offers a two-year Cisco Networking Academy that prepares students to work as Internet technicians. The program includes courses on topics such as Java programming, Unix, Web design, and information technology essentials. The courses are offered onsite and, of course, through the Internet.

About one-third of South Burlington High's students are enrolled in classes offered at the Imaging Lab. Students learn about computer-based animation, modeling, digital media development, and design. Comolli points out that his students are learning the same techniques on the same equipment used for "The Lord of the Rings" trilogy. Although a number of students are looking to the Lab experience as a prelude to a career in architecture, filmmaking, aeronautics, art, design, and medical technology, many are taking courses just for the heck of it or to become more tech-savvy in their own lives. The "mushroom people," as the students in the lab are known by their peers, are a mixed lot, but all of them are reaping the benefit of an outstanding technology experience.

Canutillo Elementary School
Canutillo, Texas

In 1998, the staff of Canutillo Elementary School (ce.canutillo. k12.tx.us/) began a two-year professional development effort through the Southwest Educational Development Laboratory's (SEDL) Technology Assistance Program (TAP). The staff began to focus on providing students with a technology-rich constructivist learning environment. Their efforts paid off handsomely, and in 2003, the school was featured in the U.S.A. Exemplary Technology-Supported Schooling Case Studies Project (http://www.edtechcases.info/schools.htm).

What makes this accomplishment all the more remarkable is that Canutillo's students face some pretty overwhelming challenges. All of the students qualified for free lunch, and many of them are not native English speakers.

The school's principal, Hector Giron, and his staff made an enormous commitment to restructuring the education environment at the school as well as to technology. About 70% of the teachers were able to participate in the TAP activities, and the remainder of the staff received their training through after-school programs and other methods. A technology committee was established to oversee the acquisition of hardware and software, and a lead teacher for instructional technology supported the integration of technology into the curriculum. At the same time, the school initiated a dual-language program because of the high number of Spanish-speaking students, and this additional innovation was worked into the technology-constructivism combination.

Although the school has a media center with networked computers, printers, and video projectors, the heart of the technology integration is within the classroom. Three or four networked computers and a printer are in each classroom, and students have access to a variety of applications such as HyperStudio, PowerPoint, Web browsing and authoring software, and Microsoft Office.

Software from Renaissance Learning, Accelerated Reader and STAR-Reading are integral to the language arts curriculum. The school sponsors a "Reading Renaissance Camp" during the summer to maintain students' reading skills. Because adult illiteracy is a problem in the area, the school keeps the library open after school so students and their parents have access to books and technology. A surprising number of parents enjoy taking Accelerated Reader quizzes after reading a book.

Even though technology and constructivism radically changed the school, the method of instruction was affected rather than the curriculum itself. The curriculum still conformed to the requirements of the TEKS (Texas Essential Knowledge and Skills) frameworks, but the content was arranged into thematic units. Students were asked to create products as part of their demonstration of knowledge, and technology was typically the vehicle for developing these products. Students might use the Internet to gather information and create a multimedia presentation using HyperStudio, usually working in pairs or collaboratively.

The Internet plays an especially important role at Canutillo because so many students come from less-wealthy homes in which information resources are not readily affordable. Through the Internet, students have access to information that would otherwise be out of their reach. The wealth of information available to students is at the heart of constructivism. As used at Canutillo, the Internet is motivating, it helps students understand that there are many things they already know, and it guides them to discover what they want to know. Moreover, it helps students apply reading and writing skills in a way that they never have before.

Although Canutillo's scores on the Texas state assessment have traditionally been low, they have improved in the last few years. Since 1994, the school has gained on average more than 50 percent, as opposed to a statewide average gain of 30 percent during the same period. These gains are even more impressive when you consider that the innovations put in place at Canutillo did not focus directly on skills assessed by the state test. Teachers report that much of the improvement can be attributed to their ability to track students' reading skills closely in both English and Spanish. They also believe that students are more excited about learning, and that their exposure to technology has given them the opportunity to develop skills they never dreamed of before.

Trey Martindale
Ward Mitchell Cates
Yufeng Qian

Analysis of Recognized Web-Based Educational Resources

SUMMARY. In 2000-2001, the authors derived a 13-category classification system for Web-based educational resources, based on analysis of 199 educational resources recognized as "exemplary" by four national entities. In 2004, we re-examined that classification system, analyzing a stratified random sample of 40 exemplary Web-based resources from the same entities. While the classification system still accommodated categorizing current educational resources, we detected some overlap among categories. Through combination and redefinition, we reduced the number of categories to eleven. This article addresses the initial and modified classification systems, the analysis procedures employed, examples of resources in each category, and future applications of the classification system. *[Article copies available for a fee from The Haworth Document Delivery Service: 1-800-HAWORTH. E-mail address: <docdelivery@haworthpress.com> Website: <http://www.HaworthPress.com> © 2004 by The Haworth Press, Inc. All rights reserved.]*

TREY MARTINDALE is Assistant Professor, Department of Librarianship, Educational Technology, and Distance Instruction, East Carolina University, Greenville, NC 27858 (E-mail: martindalee@mail.ecu.edu).
WARD MITCHELL CATES is Professor, Educational Technology Program, Lehigh University, Bethlehem, PA 18015 (E-mail: ward.cates@lehigh.edu).
YUFENG QIAN is a doctoral student, Educational Technology Program, Lehigh University, Bethlehem, PA 18015 (E-mail: yuq2@lehigh.edu).

[Haworth co-indexing entry note]: "Analysis of Recognized Web-Based Educational Resources." Martindale, Trey, Ward Mitchell Cates, and Yufeng Qian. Co-published simultaneously in *Computers in the Schools* (The Haworth Press, Inc.) Vol. 21, No. 3/4, 2004, pp. 101-117; and: *Web-Based Learning in K-12 Classrooms: Opportunities and Challenges* (ed: Jay Blanchard, and James Marshall) The Haworth Press, Inc., 2004, pp. 101-117. Single or multiple copies of this article are available for a fee from The Haworth Document Delivery Service [1-800-HAWORTH, 9:00 a.m. - 5:00 p.m. (EST). E-mail address: docdelivery@haworthpress.com].

http://www.haworthpress.com/web/CITS
Digital Object Identifier: 10.1300/J025v21n03_11

KEYWORDS. Online educational resources, classification system, educational Web site categories

The use of the Web has increased rapidly in education and has become an important resource for teaching and learning (National Center for Educational Statistics [NCES], 2003). However, the sheer number of existing Web-based educational resources can be overwhelming for educators who want to incorporate these resources into the learning activities of students. New educational resources are constantly being made available worldwide, and staying informed can be a major challenge for time-strapped educators. This challenge is compounded by the need to ensure the quality of the Web-based content in a world in which almost anyone can publish almost anything on the Web. Few individual educators can commit the time necessary to sift through thousands of resources to find the best ones for their purposes.

To assist educators and students, some organizations and agencies have recognized selected educational resources as "exemplary." For example, the International Academy of Digital Arts and Sciences (2004) selects the best resources found on the Web for the annual by Awards, and Homeschool.com (2004) annually names its top 100 educational Web-based resources. Similarly, *PC Magazine* (2004) editors annually publish a list of their top 100 Web resources, a list that includes a "learning" category. And each month the Eisenhower National Clearinghouse for Mathematics and Science Education (2004) recognizes 12 exemplary Web-based resources in science and mathematics. (Note: No effort was made on the part of the researchers to consolidate each independent agency's criteria for the definition of exemplary.) When we examined these exemplary Web-based educational resources, they found a wide variety of purposes, strategies, content, and intended audiences. The primary goals for this study were to (a) develop a system for categorizing Web-based educational resources and (b) look for trends in the types of resources most likely to be recognized as exemplary. It is noteworthy that Nachmias and Tuvi in 1998 conducted a study in which they examined the features of over 400 instructional Web-based resources. The current study may be distinguished from that effort in three ways: (a) a broader range of *educational* resources (not only *instructional*) was included, (b) all resources were chosen and examined on the basis of being designated as exemplary, and (c) a classification system of resource categories was developed.

PHASE ONE: THE INITIAL CLASSIFICATION SYSTEM

In 2001 we examined a large sample of exemplary Web-based educational resources. We compiled a list of 228 educational resources recognized by four agencies. The four agencies were the International Academy of Digital Arts and Sciences (the Webby Awards), the Eisenhower National Clearinghouse for Mathematics and Science Education (ENC), Homeschool.com, and *PC Magazine*. This sample of 228 resources represented all the educational resources recognized by these four agencies in 2000. Of the 228 resources in the sample, seven were included on more than one agency's list, including six that were recognized by three separate agencies. The lack of cross-agency agreement of what constitutes exceptional or exemplary is an indication of how varied the criteria were by the different agencies in their definitions. Sixteen of the recognized resources were no longer present online. Thus, we examined a total of 199 exemplary Web-based educational resources in the first phase of the study. From the initial stages of the analysis it was clear that the 199 resources were developed for various purposes and were diverse in terms of target audience and content. Thus, any classification system had to be broad enough to encompass the many types of resources. After a review of the resources, we drafted an initial set of categories and accompanying definitions and used these to make a preliminary analysis and classification of all the resources. We then replicated this analysis for all 199 resources, using the initial categories and definitions as guidelines. This second analysis revealed a number of differences in classification, principally due to differences in interpretation of category labels and implied definitions. As a result, the researchers refined both the categories and the definitions through discussion and negotiation.

Over several months, we debated category labels and definitions and revised the labels and definitions until they agreed on the classification. The classification system and the operational definition of each category evolved during the process of analyzing the resources. As we analyzed the resources and resolved any disagreements, the category labels and definitions in the classification system were either confirmed or modified.

Phase One: Results

Thirteen categories for Web-based educational resources emerged. Table 1 shows the 13 original categories and the distribution of the 199

TABLE 1. Distribution by Category of 199 Educational Web Sites Recognized in 2000 and Classified in 2001

Category	n	%
Content Collection	52	26.1
Instructional	40	20.1
Teacher Resource	23	11.6
Reference/Archive/News/Database (RAND)	15	7.5
Learning Activities	13	6.5
List of Links	13	6.5
Informal Education	11	5.5
Vicarious Participation	9	4.5
Virtual Exhibit	7	3.5
Research or Not-for-Profit Organization (RNO)	6	3.0
Commercial	6	3.0
Curriculum or Research Project (CRP)	2	1.0
Personal Expression and Interpersonal Interaction (PEII)	2	1.0
Totals	199	100.0

resources among them. A classified listing of all the resources can be found at http://www.coe.ecu.edu/ltdi/martindale/papers/categorize/sites.htm

Since all but two of the original 13 categories are described in subsequent sections of this article, detailed descriptions are not included here. (A detailed explanation of categories, definitions, and samples for each category is available at Martindale, Cates, and Qian, 2003.)

As Table 1 shows, the three categories with the most recognized resources were Content Collection (26.1%), Instructional (20.1%), and Teacher Resource (11.6%). These three categories accounted for almost six out of every ten resources recognized. Resources least likely to be recognized as exemplary included those in the Personal Expression and Interpersonal Interaction (PEII) category and the Curriculum or Research Project (CRP) category. Combined, these two categories accounted for only 2% of the recognized resources.

As expected, some resources could not easily be assigned to a single category. In fact, some could have been assigned to two, three, or even more categories. In dealing with multipurpose resources, we assigned each resource to the category that best fit its primary or dominant orientation, content, and purpose. For example, *NASA Is My Playground* (http://kids.msfc.nasa.gov/) and *Merriam-Webster Word Central* (http://

www.wordcentral.com) contained both instruction and teacher resources. But they contained all the elements of Instructional resources and were primarily focused on instruction, so they were classified as Instructional. *Ask Jeeves for Kids* (http://www.ajkids.com) could fit into at least three categories–RAND, Teacher Resource, and PEII. However, since the primary purpose of *Ask Jeeves for Kids* was to facilitate Web searching, it was classified as a Reference/Archive/News/Database (RAND) resource.

PHASE TWO:
VALIDATION AND REFINEMENT
OF THE CLASSIFICATION SYSTEM

The initial phase of this study was completed in 2001, with a sample of recognized Web-based educational resources from 1999 and 2000. Clearly the Web is a changing place, wishing to continue our study of how the passage of time may affect the representativeness and robustness of the classification system, we revisited the 199 resources in October 2003 and found that 14 (7%) were no longer present online. Also 13 resources (6.5%) were no longer at their original URL. Five of these resources (2.5%) provided redirect links, but 8 (4%) did not.

We decided to select a new sample of exemplary Web-based educational resources to answer two questions: (a) Are the definitions and categories of the classification system still valid (suited to categorizing Web-based educational resources)? and (b) How has the distribution of types of recognized resources changed? To answer these questions, we generated a second sample of exemplary educational resources, recognized throughout 2003, from the same four agencies: Eisenhower National Clearinghouse, Homeschool.com, the Webby Awards, and *PC Magazine*.

By October 2003, ENC had recognized 120 resources (12 per month) for the year. The Webby Awards committee had recognized 5 resources for 2003, and *PC Magazine* had recognized 16 resources in their "learning" category for 2003. Homeschool.com had recognized 100 resources from 2002, the most current year available, since their list is published at the end of the calendar year. This resulted in a total of 241 recognized resources (ENC = 50%; Webby = 2.1%; *PC Magazine* = 6.6%; Homeschool.com = 41.5%). We selected one in six of these 241 resources for analysis (16.6%) by creating a numbered list of resources from each agency and using a random number generator to select a stratified random sample from each agency in the same proportion as it was represented among the 241 total resources recognized. Thus, we selected one resource from the Webby Awards, three resources from *PC Magazine's* list, 16 resources recognized by Homeschool.com, and 20 resources from the ENC listings ($N = 40$).

As we analyzed this second set of resources, it became apparent that some original categories needed revision. For example, to resolve overlap between two category definitions, we combined Curriculum or Research Project (CRP) with Research or Non-Profit Organization (RNO) to create Research and Service Organizations and Projects (RSOP). The Teacher Resource category was renamed Teacher and Parent Resource to widen its scope. The Vicarious Participation category was changed to Shared Experiences to better address the types of resources in this category and to include resources that allowed participants to gather and submit data. This is in contrast to the former category definition, which included resources in which learners participated only peripherally in Web-based projects.

The Instructional category definition was modified to make it simpler and clearer to identify instructional resources. The Commercial category was expanded to include resources that clearly promoted products and services, or offered discounts on purchases, thus making it easier to classify commercial sites and further enhance the classification system reliability. With an overlap of the Virtual Exhibit and Informal Education categories, the former was folded into the latter. Following are the new category labels and definitions with examples of Web-based educational resources from each category.

Phase Two: Classification Categories

Instructional. To be classified as Instructional, a resource must have at least one intended learning goal or outcome and it must have learning activities that elicit a performance. It must also include some form of assessment that allows the learner to create a product, receive feedback, or reflect on the attempt to accomplish the goal(s). These instructional elements may be explicitly stated and demonstrated or they may be embedded within a resource's content.

Some Web-based resources classified as Instructional had more open-ended designs and/or exploratory navigation strategies and did not include explicitly stated learning goals. These resources did, however, incorporate learning activities that engaged learners in instructional activities that led to positive (although not necessarily prescriptive) learning outcomes. Such activities include practicing new skills; playing games; exploring related resources; searching within the resource; communicating with peers, teachers, and outside experts; exploring problem-based learning; and creating content. *How Stuff Works* (http://www.howstuffworks.com) is a good example of an *Instructional* resource from the sample.

This revised category definition eliminated some resources that contained instructional elements but were not primarily instructional in nature. For example, quizzes and educational games without instructional goals, feedback, or assessment were not categorized as Instructional. We found it important to avoid being misled by the labels for some resources. For example, some resources with content labels such as *tutorial* or *problem-based learning project* appeared at first perusal to fit the Instructional category but did not in fact meet the requirements of our definition. *Embryo Images* (http://www.med.unc.edu/embryo_images/) is an example of a resource that initially appeared to be Instructional but was not. While the resource was touted to as an instructional tutorial, it was simply a slide show of images with text captions and failed to include intended learning goals or assessment. Similarly, *The ART Room* (http://www.arts.ufl.edu/art/rt_room/index.html) contained valuable content for learning about art but had no instructional goals or assessment.

Learning Activities. Learning Activities resources are intended for learners (as opposed to teachers or parents) and feature learning activities and/or educational games to be downloaded or completed online. These activities may be incorporated into the classroom, lab, or distance learning curricula, but do not exhibit the components of Instructional resources (intended learning goals and assessment or opportunity for reflection). *Physics and Calculus Problems of the Week* (http://www.kent.wednet.edu/pcpow/), a resource for secondary students featuring weekly problems and solutions from math and calculus, is a well-designed Learning Activities resource that could contribute to learning both inside and outside the classroom. It did not, however, qualify as an Instructional resource because it had neither intended goals nor assessment. *Village Math* (http://www.ankn.uaf.edu/VillageMath/village_math.html) is another Learning Activities resource containing math problems for students based on real-life scenarios from village life in northern Canada and Alaska.

Content Collection. A resource classified as a Content Collection is a compilation of information about a specific content area (e.g., genetics, coaching basketball, the works of Shakespeare). Such resources often include informative readings, illustrations, and other rich content. They are not classified as Instructional because they do not include intended learning goals or assessment, nor are they Learning Activities, as they do not include active learner participation. While a Content Collection resource may feature a few external hyperlinks, by this classification system it should consist primarily of within-site content. If a resource contains primarily external links rather than internal content, it is classified as a List of Links (see next category). An example of a Content Collection resource is *Common Cold* (http://www.commoncold.org/), a comprehensive source of information about the common cold. Another example is *The European Middle Ages* (http://www.wsu.edu/~dee/ MA/MA.HTM).

List of Links. A resource in this category features organized external links to resources about a topic or theme. The resource should serve principally as an index for external content and should contain little or no original content of its own. If a resource's links are mostly internal (i.e., most of the actual content is located within the resource itself), it should be classified as a Content Collection or RAND, depending on its other characteristics. *European Renaissance* (http://www.execpc.com/~ dboals/rena.html) is a good example of a List of Links, with 67 external links related to the Renaissance.

Reference/Archive/News/Database (RAND). These Web-based resources offer access to reference tools (such an encyclopedia, dictionary, or atlas), archives of content with potential educational value, news, and databases that might prove useful to teachers or learners. These resources may be indexed chronologically, alphabetically, or topically and are designed as information and reference tools. Web-based news agencies, encyclopedias, reference books, and question-answer services belong in this category. RAND resources differ from Content Collections and Lists of Links because they are broader, may address multiple topics, and are oriented toward searching for information rather than examining collected information related to a specific topic. One example of a RAND resource is *Footnotes to History* (http://www.buckyogi.com/footnotes/index.htm), a Web-based encyclopedia of nations and states from world history. *CNN Interactive* (http://www.cnn.com) represents a news-based RAND resource, while *The Last Word Science Questions and Answers* (http://www.lastword.com/) and *Ask Jeeves for Kids* (http://www.ajkids.com/) represented question-and-answer RAND resources. An example of a resource that appeared by title to be a RAND site–but was not–was *Math Dictionary for Kids* (http://www.amathsdictionaryforkids.com/). Despite its title, this resource actually qualified as a Learning Activities resource, as it went well beyond being Web-based dictionary by providing engaging learning activities.

Teacher and Parent Resources. Teacher and Parent Resources (TPR) are designed to provide instructors or parents with lesson plans, instructor guides, or home-schooling materials. These materials may be displayed online, or available as downloadable files. While such resources may also include subject matter links and learner activities, the main focus is assisting teachers or parents, and this is usually reflected in the language used within the resource. Such resources often address teachers directly with phrases such as "your students" and "your classes." Note that if a resource is primarily for teacher professional development, or deals with larger curricular issues or national standards, it is classified as a Research and Service Organizations and Projects (RSOP).

One example of a TPR, *Illuminations* (http://illuminations.nctm.org/), offers online multimedia math investigations, classroom video vignettes, standards-based lesson plans, and links to reviewed Web sites. Another TPR is *Teaching Plastics* (http://www.teachingplastics.org/). It offers activities for young students to help them understand plastics.

Shared Experiences. A Shared Experiences resource provides learners with opportunities to take part online in ongoing educational or research activities and expeditions, including virtual field trips. Resources representing projects in which participants actually gather data and can post it to a central database are also included in this category. (These are sometimes called *collaborative Web-based experiments.*) An example of such an experiment in our sample is *eBird* (http://www.ebird.org).

Shared Experiences resources attempt to give the learner a sense of participation in activities not typically available in the classroom. Such resources often contain archival materials from past explorations for educational use after the activity is concluded. In *Extreme 2000* (http://www.ocean.udel.edu/deepsea/), a deep-sea research expedition, learners view video clips of the expedition, read the dive log and daily journal, send e-mail messages to the researchers, and listen to live audio from the research team. Similarly, in *The Jason Project* (http://www.jasonproject.org/) learners participate in an ongoing expedition and also use resources and learn from past expeditions.

Personal Expression and Interpersonal Interaction. Resources classified as Personal Expression and Interpersonal Interaction (PEII) are those designed to facilitate discussion, interaction, and other types of information sharing. A PEII resource differs from a Shared Experiences resource in that the former exists to encourage personal connection and interaction among students, while the latter emphasizes educational content in the form of research projects or virtual field trips. PEII users might, for example, play interactive games and share thoughts and ideas with one another via e-mail, chat, and/or message boards. These resources usually do not include learning activities, although they may be classified as educational in the broader sense if they encourage discussion of events and issues important to learners. Sample PEII sites include *It's Your Turn Online Games* (http://www.itsyourturn.com), where participants play various logic games and exchange tips with other participants, and *Kids Space* (http://www.kids-space.org/), an area for interaction and discussion.

Informal Education. These resources represent actual places such as zoos, museums, historic sites, gardens, aquaria, and parks that have an educational component. This category also includes real-world or virtual exhibits. Informal Education resources often include content such as visitor information, schedules, exhibit information, maps and directions, membership and funding information, and special events. Resources in this category may offer an education section with learning materials and activities for teachers and students. *Exploratorium* (http://www.exploratorium.edu/index.html) and *Colonial Williamsburg* (http://www.history.org) are good examples of Informal Education resources.

Research and Service Organizations and Projects (RSOP). A resource in this category represents a particular research, academic, or service organization. Also included are short-term and long-term research, service, or curricular projects designed to aid educational endeavors. An RSOP resource typically addresses the nature and purpose of an organization, current and past projects, recent results, news and events, and related educational materials and activities. Three NASA resources that typify RSOP sites are *NASA* (http://www.nasa.gov/), the *NASA Jet Propulsion Laboratory* (http://www.jpl.nasa.gov), and the *Sun-Earth Forum* (http://sunearth.gsfc.nasa.gov/). RSOP resources differ from those in other categories, such as Teacher and Parent Resources, because their content focuses on a particular project of the host organization.

Commercial. Commercial resources are primarily intended to promote and sell products or services. Such resources often include additional components designed to inform, educate, or entertain, and may be quite rich in terms of educational content. For example, a company selling diabetes medication might include information or instruction about the causes and treatments of diabetes. One can often recognize a commercial resource by the presence of a shopping cart, links to purchase products or services, or advertisements for discounts on purchases (see, for example, Do It Yourself (http://doityourself.com). Some Commercial resources, such as *Foreign Languages for Travelers* (http://www.travlang. com/languages), are so aggressive in promoting their products that their educational content is overshadowed.

It is sometimes necessary to explore a resource extensively to identify it as primarily Commercial in nature. The presence of sponsorship (as indicated by advertising) does not necessarily mean a resource should be classified as Commercial, since advertising may be a way for educational resources to maintain viability. Other examples of Commercial resources included *SurfMonkey Kids Channel* (http://www. surfmonkey.com/) and *U.S. Space Camp* (http://www.spacecamp.com).

Phase Two: Results

Once the labels and definitions of categories were improved and clarified, we independently analyzed the 40 resources in the sample based on the refined classification system and collaboratively evaluated and analyzed the resources to reach complete agreement on how each resource should be classified. Table 2 shows the distribution of this final classification.

As seen in Table 2, Commercial resources were the most prevalent in the sample of 40 (20%). This represents quite a change from Phase One,

TABLE 2. Distribution by Category of 40 Educational Web Sites Recognized in 2003

Category	n	%
Commercial	8	20
Content Collection	6	15
Instructional	4	10
Teacher and Parent Resource (TPR)	4	10
Research and Service Organizations and Projects (RSOP)	4	10
Informal Education	4	10
Reference/Archive/News/Database (RAND)	3	7.5
Learning Activities	3	7.5
List of Links	2	5
Shared Experiences	1	2.5
Personal Expression and Interpersonal Interaction (PEII)	1	2.5
Totals	40	100.0

in which only 3% of the resources were classified as Commercial. Content Collections were the second most common category, accounting for 15% of the sample. This was followed by four other categories, each representing four resources (10%).

CONCLUSION

Looking back on Phase One findings, only one in five (20%) of the 199 recognized resources was primarily instructional in nature. Conversely, four of every five resources were not primarily instructional, although the agencies judged them as educational in the broadest sense. The substantial presence (26%) of Content Collections in the first sample suggests that the agencies at that time placed great importance on high-quality content and materials for use by teachers and students in learning. Similarly, the large number of Teacher Resources in the sample ($n = 25$) suggests that recognizing agencies viewed such resources as key to the educational enterprise.

Six of the top seven categories represented areas commonly seen as falling within the educational venue. Content Collection, Instructional, Teacher Resource, RAND, Learning Activities, and Informal Education resources all map easily onto the framework of traditional education. Even the sixth of these seven categories (Lists of Links) fits, since such resources frequently provide links to the other six types of resources. Thus, Lists of Links represents a way of helping users organize more focused sets of resources in key classifications, often for the purpose of studying particular content (for example, the Civil War).

In the frequency distribution, the bottom six categories accounted for only 16% of all recognized Web-based resources. These categories may represent a less conventional understanding of what is educational. That is, resources in these categories may represent entities or activities not traditionally viewed as falling within the educational venue.

In examining the Phase Two findings, we found the distribution across categories had changed. However, this may have been due in part to the redefinition of some categories and to two categories being subsumed by others. Despite some reordering, the categories that represented areas commonly falling within the educational venue once again accounted for large numbers of recognized resources. Content Collections still accounted for a large proportion of the recognized resources, followed closely by Instructional and Teacher and Parent Resources.

Even when one looks at the Commercial resources, the major difference may not be greater prevalence or increased recognition by the four agencies, but rather the extent to which electronic commerce has made commercial intentions more apparent (through prominently displayed online shopping carts, for instance). Creating an online store to sell products has also become dramatically simpler, to the point that any individual or group can have an online store. Services such as *CafePress* (http://www.cafepress.com) handle every aspect of running an online store for any group, for a share of the sales revenue. So there has been a decrease in the technical barriers to electronic commerce, just as there has been a simultaneous increase in the acceptance of electronic commerce by the general public.

When the authors analyzed the first set of resources (only a few months after the 215 resources were recognized by the various agencies), 16 of the recognized resources (7.4%) were no longer available online. These resources were either moved without notice or a forwarding URL, or discontinued despite recognition as exemplary educational resources. Now three years later, as noted earlier, an additional 14 Web-based resources were gone, bringing the total attrition to 30 resources (14.0%). In addition, the eight resources with URLs that had changed without redirection notice would be unavailable to many users who might not know to how locate them, raising that total to 38, or better than one in six. This finding reinforces how rapidly things change on the Web, and may suggest a tenuous link between educational excellence and economic viability for these recognized Web-based resources. That is, some resources recognized as exemplary may not be self-sustaining, and exemplary resources that do not have sufficient internal or external backing or sponsorship may be discontinued. This may also help account for the greater prevalence of Commercial resources on the 2003 listings. In the business world this is commonly referred to as a "shake-out." That is, in a crowded market, commercially viable organizations or products succeed, while those operating under less effective business models fail.

While this classification system did not focus on the technical components of Web-based resource construction, we did observe that technical demands may well dictate what appears online. Clearly it is technically much simpler to create a list of links than a highly interactive instructional resource or an open-ended learning environment. Personal Expression and Interpersonal Interaction resources appeared much less frequently on lists of "exemplary" resources, and these resources require more expertise to create and significantly more time to manage. That said, we did note that a number of recognized resources exhibited technical sophistication.

Recognized exemplary resources often exhibited solid production values. That is, they had better-than-average appearance (graphic design) and functionality (interface design, navigation, usability). Thus, aesthetic appeal may have played a role in some resources making the exemplary lists. For an example of such recognized high-quality production values and functionality, see *Froguts* (http://www.froguts. com/).

The Web is an evolving entity, with constantly improving editing tools, scripting languages, protocols, plug-ins, and standards. And both professional designers and novice Web publishers are becoming more proficient and capable, even as Web access and use become increasingly ubiquitous. In terms of design and technical capability, what was nearly impossible two years ago became difficult last year and is routine today. We noted evidence of this growth in capability in comparing the two samples. Certainly Web-based educational resources will continue to evolve as technologies advance and more educators and other publishers bring content online. While any classification system may represent a trailing indicator of current practice in the design and use of Web-based educational resources, the system derived and presented here should prove relatively independent of the technology employed. What will likely change, however, is the distribution of exemplary resources across these categories, as technical sophistication becomes more commonplace. The Web is increasingly being recognized and employed for communication as opposed to mere distribution of content.

Given that Instructional resources account for 44 of the 239 resources in the two samples (18.4%), what we found in terms of design philosophy warrants some discussion. The Web has received much attention as a potential medium for creating constructivist learning environments (Land & Greene, 2000; Reeves & Reeves, 1997; Stepich & Ertmer, 2003; Tan & Hung, 2002; Wilson, 1997; Wilson & Lowry, 2000). A constructivist view generally posits that (a) knowledge is constructed, not transmitted; (b) knowledge construction results from activity; (c) knowledge is embedded in activity; (d) meaning is in the mind of the knower; and (e) there are multiple perspectives on the world, within which the learner constructs reality (Christensen, 2003; Ertmer & Newby, 1993; Hannafin, Hannafin, Land, & Oliver, 1997; Jonassen, Peck, & Wilson, 1999; Perkins, 1991; Wu, 2003; Duffy, Lowyck, Jonassen, & NATO Advanced Research Workshop on the Design of Constructivist Learning Environments: Implications for Instructional Design and the Use of Technology, 1993). However, most of the recognized exemplary Instructional resources appeared to reflect a cognitive or behavioral instructional design. These designs reflect a theoretical orientation that (a) knowledge is stable, fixed, and can be transmitted; (b) knowledge and reality are external to the knower; and (c) well-structured instructor-led events and strategies facilitate encoding, retention, and retrieval of knowledge (Dick, 1996; Hannafin & Rieber, 1989; Roblyer, 1996).

The lack of constructivist exemplars in the sample is consistent with the findings of Mioduser, Nachmias, Lahav, and Oren (2000) whose investigation of 436 Web-based educational resources revealed limited pedagogical diversity. Resources examined in their study often employed drill-and-practice and direct instruction as primary instructional strategies. It is unclear whether this finding is inextricably tied to technical concerns, however. That is, it is substantially more difficult to create Web-based resources that accommodate the demands of constructivist learning, including such things as teamwork, sharing of products, facilitating communities of practice, participating in projects of more knowledgeable peers and experts, and the like. As the capabilities of the Web and its designers and developers evolve, educators may see more constructivist principles employed.

It appears that the classification system proposed, as refined in the second phase, accommodates a wide range of educational resources and should prove useful to teachers and parents, and perhaps recognizing agencies. An additional promising use of this classification system might be in the design of Web portals, thus making clearer to potential users the nature of what given resources offer. (A Web portal is a Web site that offers users a starting point for pursuing an area of interest across the Web. Lists of Links represent one basic type of Web portal.)

Future researchers may wish to expand on these resource categories, creating more detailed sub-categorizations. Such expansion could, in turn, provide further specificity for Web portal linkages. In addition, future researchers might wish to explore technical features and properties of exemplary resources as a way of refining our understanding of what role such factors as production values and technical sophistication play in a resource being recognized.

REFERENCES

Christensen, T. (2003). Case 1: Finding the balance: Constructivist pedagogy in a blended course. *Quarterly Review of Distance Education, 4*(3), 235-243.

Dick, W. (1996). The Dick and Carey model: Will it survive the decade? *Educational Technology Research and Development, 44*(3), 55-63.

Duffy, T., Lowyck, J., Jonassen, D., & NATO Advanced Research Workshop on the Design of Constructivist Learning Environments: Implications for Instructional Design and the Use of Technology. (1993). *Designing environments for constructive learning.* Berlin: Springer-Verlag.

Eisenhower National Clearinghouse for Mathematics and Science Education. (2004). *Digital dozen.* Retrieved July 1, 2004, from http://www.enc.org/Weblinks/dd/

Ertmer, P., & Newby, T. (1993). Behaviorism, cognitivism, constructivism: Comparing critical features from an instructional design perspective. *Performance Improvement Quarterly, 6*(2), 50-72.

Hannafin, M. J., Hannafin, K. M., Land, S., & Oliver, K. (1997). Grounded practice and the design of constructivist learning environments. *Educational Technology Research and Development, 45*(3), 101-117.

Hannafin, M., & Rieber, L. (1989). Psychological foundations of instructional design for emerging computer-based instructional technologies: Parts I and II. *Educational Technology Research and Development, 37*(2), 91-114.

Homeschool.com (2004). *Top 100 educational Websites.* Retrieved July 15, 2004, from http://www.homeschool.com/top100/

International Academy of Digital Arts and Sciences. (2004). *Webby awards.* Retrieved June 10, 2004, from http://www.Webbyawards.com/main/

Jonassen, D., Peck, K., & Wilson, B. (1999). *Learning with technology: A constructivist perspective.* Upper Saddle River, NJ: Merrill.

Land, S., & Greene, B. (2000). Project-based learning with the World Wide Web: A qualitative study of resource integration. *Educational Technology Research and Development, 48*(1), 45-67.

Martindale, T., Cates, W., & Qian, Y. (2003). Educational Web sites: A classification system for educators and learners. *Educational Technology, 43*(6), 47-50.

Mioduser, D., Nachmias, R., Lahav, O., & Oren, A. (2000). Web-based learning environments: Current pedagogical and technological state. *Journal of Research on Computing in Education, 33*(1), 55-76.

National Center for Education Statistics (2003). *Distance education at degree-granting postsecondary institutions: 2000-2001.* (NCES 2003-017). Washington, DC: U.S. Department of Education.

Nachmias, R., & Tuvi, I. (1998). Taxonomy of scientifically oriented educational Websites. Retrieved April 15, 2004, from http://muse.tau.ac.il/publications/76.pdf

PC Magazine. (2004). 100 top Websites you didn't know you couldn't live without. Retrieved July 1, 2004, from http://www.pcmag.com/article2/0,1759,1554010,00.asp

Perkins, D. (1991). Technology meets constructivism: Do they make a marriage? *Educational Technology, 31*(5), 18-23.

Reeves, T. C., & Reeves, P. C. (1997). Effective dimensions of interactive learning on the World Wide Web. In B. Khan (Ed.), *Web-based instruction* (pp. 59-66). Englewood Cliffs, NJ: Educational Technology Publications.

Roblyer, M. (1996). The constructivist/objectivist debate: Implications for instructional technology research. *Learning and Leading with Technology, 24*(2), 12-16.

Stepich, D., & Ertmer, P. (2003). Building community as a critical element of online course design. *Educational Technology, 43*(5), 33-43.

Tan, S., & Hung, D. (2002). Beyond information pumping: Creating a constructivist e-learning environment. *Educational Technology, 42*(5), 48-54.

Wilson, B., & Lowry, M. (2000). Constructivist learning on the Web. Retrieved July 15, 2004, from http://ceo.cudenver.edu/~brent_wilson/WebLearning.html

Wilson, B. (1997). Reflections on constructivism and instructional design. In C. Dills & A. Romiszowski (Eds.), *Instructional development paradigms* (pp. 63-80). Englewood Cliffs, NJ: Educational Technology Publications.

Wu, A. (2003). Supporting electronic discourse: Principles of design from a social constructivist perspective. *Journal of Interactive Learning Research, 14*(2), 167-184.

James Marshall

Implementation and Web-Based Learning: The Unimplemented Program Yields Few Results

SUMMARY. This paper turns away from Web-based learning content and addresses a universal concern of technology-based learning, namely, program implementation. Without the necessary attention to curriculum alignment, implementation planning and support, Web-based learning initiatives can fall victim to competing priorities. Here, we present the ATLAS model which has been designed to guide program planning and implementation. *[Article copies available for a fee from The Haworth Document Delivery Service: 1-800-HAWORTH. E-mail address: <docdelivery@ haworthpress.com> Website: <http://www.HaworthPress.com> © 2004 by The Haworth Press, Inc. All rights reserved.]*

KEYWORDS. Implementation, technology, curriculum, e-learning, evaluation, alignment, needs assessment, planning, results

"What makes a new subject in school most interesting to you?" In 2001, *USA Today* posed this question to children ages 6 to 11. The re-

JAMES MARSHALL is an Adjunct Faculty Member, Department of Educational Technology, San Diego State University, San Diego, CA 92103 (E-mail: marshall@ mail.sdsu.edu).

[Haworth co-indexing entry note]: "Implementation and Web-Based Learning: The Unimplemented Program Yields Few Results." Marshall, James. Co-published simultaneously in *Computers in the Schools* (The Haworth Press, Inc.) Vol. 21, No. 3/4, 2004, pp. 119-129; and: *Web-Based Learning in K-12 Classrooms: Opportunities and Challenges* (ed: Jay Blanchard, and James Marshall) The Haworth Press, Inc., 2004, pp. 119-129. Single or multiple copies of this article are available for a fee from The Haworth Document Delivery Service [1-800-HAWORTH, 9:00 a.m. - 5:00 p.m. (EST). E-mail address: docdelivery@haworthpress.com].

Digital Object Identifier: 10.1300/J025v21n03_12

sults surprised some: 34% indicated the Internet; 24%, television; and teacher and textbook received 26% and 12%, respectively. These results are good news for e-learning advocates; students like technology. But favor does not necessarily yield results.

The worldwide accountability movement has increased emphasis on documented results. For example, in the United States, the federal government "suggests" methods and materials that can be used for teaching and learning through the *What Works Clearinghouse* (www.w-w-c. org). The idea is to identify programs and products that, when employed purposefully, bring about predictable results and then to document those results. Web-based learning resources face the same scrutiny.

This paper focuses on a single element of this idea-purposeful implementation of Web-based learning programs. Fifteen years of developing technology-based learning products and evaluating their use in schools has revealed one unequivocal truth to this author: The unused program yields few results. While content developers, school districts, and grant programs alike invest their capital into instructional programs and evaluation studies, one outcome is clear: The unimplemented program becomes a study about what *could* have happened and why it did not–rather than increasing our understanding of what works, what doesn't, and why. Purposeful implementation is prerequisite to both student learning and achievement, *and* to judging the effectiveness of Web-based learning programs.

SUPPORTING IMPLEMENTATION

What can be done to increase the chances of successful program implementation? This paper presents a model, dubbed ATLAS, for program implementation–from planning through ongoing evaluation. Our focus rests on larger technology implementations: schoolwide e-learning programs, integrated learning systems, or technology-based professional development. However, the model's generalizability to selection of instructional materials large and small, including non-technology solutions, could easily be made. Two examples of the ATLAS model applied to current Web-based learning endeavors–an integrated learning system implementation in Charlotte County, Florida, and the development and implementation of C-SPAN-provided resources in New York–are also featured.

Picture a technology-based program currently being used in your world. Trace back the program's history. How did it come to reside in your district, school, or classroom? Is it being used to full potential? Perhaps one of the following rationale in responsible, in whole or part, for its presence.

- I saw it at the tech conference and it was great . . . so we're getting it for every teacher.
- This thing is great—it's a reading-mathematics-science program all rolled into one. Our test scores are going to go up in every area!
- How are we supposed to use this online program? Our Internet connection works half the time and, even then, my dial-up line at home is faster.
- I know the program is successful—the kids love it.
- We tried that last year, it kind of worked . . . this year we're going to do something totally different.

Purposeful implementation of Web-based learning programs begins with matching the program to a specific need. It continues with assessing and optimizing the program to better meet teacher and student needs. The ATLAS model is a reaction to comments such as those listed and is a framework to guide implementation planning and action. Table 1 presents its five components.

ATLAS MODEL

Alignment

Today's climate of high stakes testing and accountability has focused teachers' efforts on achieving standards. Products and programs that do not contribute to these efforts increasingly receive less attention. Alignment between technology-based programs, standards and specific school or district needs is the foundation of a successful implementation. It ensures the program is *relevant* to the needs of everyone involved.

How does this alignment process begin? Start by identifying opportunities—and priorities. That likely involves reviewing data—test scores, school performance, current programs. It definitely means dialoging with teachers.

ATLAS is predicated on shared-decision making. The need for teachers to be involved in instructional material decisions is well documented (Bauer, 1992; Kirby, 1992; Odden & Busch, 1998). Teacher participation in selection and implementation planning insures implementation. Programs that follow a "B-52" implementation model—

TABLE 1. ATLAS Model

Component	Questions to Guide Implementation
Align–with district, school, and/or classroom initiatives	• What are your current instructional priorities and needs? • What priorities are not being met sufficiently? Where do gaps exist? • Is technology a good match to this need? • Are these shared priorities between administration and teachers?
Target–the program's size and participant effort	• How will the program be phased in? • What is a reasonable implementation expectation for teachers and their students? • How can the program be scaled up over time?
Leverage–resources and support for teachers and students	• How will teachers learn to use the program–and plan for its implementation? • Will teachers be motivated to implement the program? Think time, reward, and recognition in addition to monetary. • When problems occur, who will teachers turn to? • How will teachers collaborate with peers to optimize their implementations and problem solve? • Do teachers have the necessary technology to implement the program? • Are students able to access and operate the technology at the requisite level?
Asses–the program outcomes over time	• What indicators will signal program success? • How will teachers monitor the success of the program in their classrooms?
Sustain–the program long enough to gain results and optimize implementation	• How will data be used to monitor the program over time? • How will the program be adjusted and honed based upon results? Consider teacher and student perspectives. • Are expectations realistic for the defined implementation period? For future scaling of the program?

where materials are "dropped" into the school and implementation is as-sumed–often result in program materials, shrink-wrap unbroken, come school-year end.

Bringing teachers to the table at the start to tap their expertise makes sense. The benefits of this process are many. They reach beyond imple-mentation to encompass each teacher's personal development. Speak-ing solely to implementation, teacher involvement insures alignment with frontline needs and produces program advocates from the start.

Target

Schools, teachers, and students alike are barraged with conflicting priorities, immediate needs, and competing distractions. These everyday realities can quickly make just completing the instructional day overwhelming. Technology-based programs are frequently adopted with an eye to simplifying the lives of teachers. In practice, e-learning implementations can achieve the opposite result by complicating and overwhelming everyone involved.

Targeting the implementation addresses teacher confidence that the teachers indeed *can* successfully implement the program. This focus naturally complements relevance established by the alignment process. Together they contribute to the performance of participants (Lawler & Porter, 1967; Rossett, 1999). Even the most relevant program will fail to be implemented if teachers don't believe they will be successful.

Targeting is the process of setting realistic goals. Implementers set realistic expectations of what teachers can accomplish in each phase of the implementation process and build upon that foundation as implementation expands.

For example, rather than implementing a program districtwide, start with a manageable pilot and promote its success (see Charlotte County example). Also, focus the initial implementation of a reading program on a priority need–for example, reading comprehension. Then, with success, expand its use to other areas.

Leverage

Barriers to successful implementation are inevitable. The motivation to implement the program shares an inverse relationship with barriers. Said another way, when difficult problems arise, motivation levels fall. This is where leveraging available resources and support becomes critical. Webster defines leveraging as the "act of providing or supplementing." Consider the following opportunities for leveraging that can make or break a program's implementation.

Troubleshooting. Program implementers are given access to troubleshooting help–both technical and content-related (also see Training).

Technology. While it may seem obvious, the requisite technology must be available to teacher and student users whenever they initiate use. Unreliable access, or low-performing technologies will quickly affect use.

Training. Teachers develop familiarity with the program. Access to program developers or expert users helps teachers continue to increase their program expertise. Likewise, teachers are able to instruct students and facilitate successful program use.

Time. Time is a finite commodity. If teachers are expected to implement a program, they must be given dedicated, compensated time to develop familiarity and plan classroom use. Planned time for collaboration with peers may also be a beneficial way to support program use.

Measure

It has been said, "What's measured matters." This adage rings especially true in our schools. Witness the attention to standards aligned with state tests. Since alignment with a specific need or set of challenges forms the basis of program selection, it is natural to follow through by measuring ongoing progress toward meeting that need or solving the set of challenges (see CIPP framework: Stufflebeam, 2000; Worthen, Sanders, & Fitzpatrick, 1997).

At the classroom level, continuous monitoring and assessment accomplished by participating teachers have roles to play beyond measuring individual student progress. Looking at classroom data compared to program use–even informally–can provide insight into program use and results. Likewise, this type of monitoring can also be used to individualize program use based on student needs.

Many technology-based programs provide a host of reports and usage data for program monitoring. While valuable, the sheer volume of data can be overwhelming. Here again, targeting results can help. Teachers can select one or two specific variables to track on a regular basis. Perhaps the variable is level of mastery on specific objectives, or number of units completed at mastery level. The point is to use data to monitor learning; tailor the use of technology to individual student needs; and make ongoing, formative judgments about program success.

With the myriad achievement measures available to educators today, it makes sense to evaluate program results in light of student achievement. At the school or district level, measuring student achievement results in light of factors such as program use (time on task, number of units/lesson/modules completed, etc.) broadens the results picture. Yet, don't underestimate the power of talking to the people using the program. For teachers, what do they see happening in their classrooms? For students, what have they learned? These informal reflections can color and instantiate quantitative trends identified through test scores and other aggregate, summative measures.

Whether assessing at the classroom, school, or district level, the purpose of this ATLAS component's presence is to measure worth. That means taking stock of what you set out to accomplish compared to where you currently stand–and basing your judgments on data.

Sustain

Program adjustments are a fact of school life–especially in the face of rigorous measurement and increasing pressure to perform. Yet, results take time to realize. Expectations for program results should be realistic and established for both short-term and long-term timeframes.

Begin by setting a realistic outcome for the initial implementation period. During this period, results from assessment activities are considered and the program is adjusted to better meet the needs of teacher and student alike. This continuous improvement cycle is repeated as the implementation expands and provides the opportunity to hone implementations and self-correct where necessary.

If you have taken the time to align the program to a critical need, and planned and supported implementation, yet formative results are unfavorable, abandoning the program is but one of many options. While often the simplest option, it quickly yields the cynicism inherent in "projectitis" and "flavor of the month." Clearly, if a program proves to have no potential for impact, abandonment may make sense. But consider sustaining the program to gather feedback and data, further develop and support participants, and make necessary adjustments. This process of exacting the implementation may indeed advance you closer to your goal.

ATLAS Applied

The ATLAS model is based upon theory, practice, and common sense. The intent is to provide an applied framework that can guide program implementation. While the model remains to be formally tested, the following two examples align each ATLAS model component with successful e-learning implementations.

New York School Districts: The Points of View Project. Funded by a Cable in the Classroom grant, Points of View (POV) combines teacher expertise, cable programming and resources (C-SPAN, the History Channel), videoconferencing capabilities (Cable in the Classroom online tools), high-speed Internet service (Time Warner Cable) into an inquiry-based curriculum centered on the life and presidency of Theodore Roosevelt. Master teachers from four New York school districts (Schenectady, Amsterdam, Ballston Spa, and Scotia/Glenville) created a model for interactive teaching and learning that fosters analytic thinking. Direct broadband access to primary documents, streaming video, and live interaction via videoconferencing with experts make for a dynamic curriculum which is available online and can be used by teachers and students in any K-12 classroom. See www.c-span.org/classroom/pov/pov_home.asp (Figure 1).

Evaluation results indicate that Points of View students reliably outperformed students in a matched comparison group. Why has this implementation succeeded–and produced measurable results? Consider the project attributes in light of the ATLAS model. Table 2 articulates project attributes aligned to the implementation model components.

Collaboration between the people who are ultimately responsible for the project's implementation is at the heart of this e-learning venture.

FIGURE 1. Points of View Website

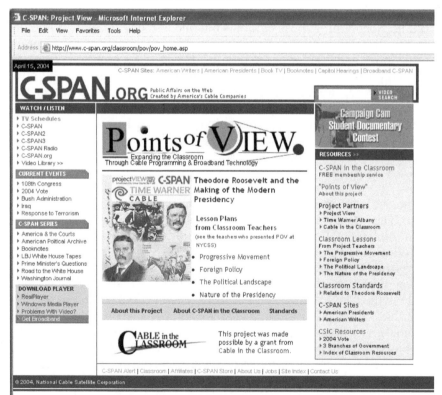

TABLE 2. Points of View Implementation Features

Component	Points of VIEW Project Feature
Align–with district, school, and/or classroom initiatives	• Teachers played significant roles that included: identifying themes and content, designing the curriculum model and developing the curriculum. • Project content aligns with New York state standards and is tested on the state assessment.
Target–the program's size and participant effort	• POV focused on developing a curriculum model and testing it with a slice of relevant content (Presidency of Theodore Roosevelt). • POV *did not* set out to create a large, unrealistic number of lessons in multiple content areas.
Leverage–resources and support for teachers and students	• Teachers were provided time to create lessons and plan implementation. • Project partners assisted teachers in planning and implementation. • Opportunities to showcase work and results were provided and encouraged.
Assess–the program outcomes over time	• Measures for project success were identified at the start. They included teacher outcomes (model and curriculum development) and cognitive outcomes (student performance on questions modeled after the state test). • Regular collaboration with evaluators' guided implementation and documented project outcomes.
Sustain–the program long enough to gain results and optimize implementation	• Positive results from measurement of the pilot validate the model. • Results establish the program's efficacy. This, in turn, justifies and motivates expanded use.

C-SPAN content experts worked hand in hand with teachers to design the implementation model and curriculum. With such intimate involvement in the process, it is no surprise POV was implemented in each participating classroom.

Charlotte County Public Schools and Compass Learning. In 2001, the Charlotte County Public Schools, Port Charlotte, Florida (http://www.ccps.k12.fl.us), set out to adopt Web-based learning system to support student achievement. A desired feature of this system would be after-school home access for students, in addition to the traditional classroom. Table 3 highlights components of Charlotte County's implementation model correlated to the ATLAS model.

From the start, Charlotte County involved teachers in program selection and implementation design. The district's elementary schools competed to become pilot sites through a Request for Proposal (RFP) process. Through this activity the schools defined their implementation

TABLE 3. Charlotte County–CompassLearning Implementation Features

Component	Charlotte County Project Feature
Align–with district, school, and/or classroom initiatives	• A curriculum selection committee–including teachers, curriculum and instructional specialists, school-based leadership, and district level leaders–reviewed products and selected the implemented product. • Product selection criteria was identified based upon district priorities, including: – Content breadth, alignment, and quality – Ease of use – Availability of technology for home and school use
Target–the program's size and participant effort	• While the program will eventually be used in each school, the pilot implementation targeted three schools. Schools responded to a Request for Proposal (RFP) from the district by defining: – Grade levels they would implement – How licenses would be distributed – How both home and school use would be encouraged • Charlotte County *did not* roll the program out to the entire district.
Leverage–resources and support for teachers and students	• Teachers were provided training and support from CompassLearning consultants throughout the pilot implementation. • The district's Department of Learning Through Technology, school-based facilitators and Compass Learning representatives worked hand in hand to facilitate the pilot implementation and smooth inevitable bumps along the way. • District leaders visited schools, consulted with teachers and monitored progress.
Assess–the program outcomes over time	• Assessment of the pilot tracked student usage statistics–measured by the technology and participant feedback. • Goals related to time on task were set and each school was measured against that goal. Pilot school access to the e-learning program was adjusted based upon use. • Future assessment will continue usage measurement. It will expand to cognitive outcomes, including: – Evaluating student use of the technology against performance on statewide tests. – Investigating whether performance on the CompassLearning assessments predicts performance.
Sustain–the program long enough to gain results and optimize implementation	• Charlotte County benefited from the pilot period. Lessons learned here will ease the program's expansion to an additional seven elementary schools.

and demonstrated how defined implementation objectives would be met.

This e-learning implementation included a notable usage incentive. Charlotte County purchased a limited number of student licenses. Practically, this meant the number of students exceeded the number of licenses. To reinforce use during the pilot period, student use at each pilot school was tracked, and the allocation of licenses was adjusted based upon these statistics.

While initial assessment centers upon usage statistics and user feedback, ongoing measurement will tie program use and performance to statewide accountability measures. This complementary data will inform implementation as the program continues to expand throughout the district.

ATLAS and the Future

The ATLAS model is a useful, practical typology that guides implementation–from planning through actual use. It places emphasis on five components that strongly influence the success of any program's implementation.

While the ATLAS model is based upon theory, practice, and common sense, it remains untested in practice. Future efforts must focus on model validation through its use for implementation planning.

REFERENCES

Bauer, S. (1992). Myth, consensus, and change. *Executive Educator, 14*(7), 26-28.

Kirby, P. C. (1992). Shared decision making: Moving from concerns about restrooms to concerns about classrooms. *Journal of School Leadership, 2*(3), 330-344.

Lawler, E., & Porter, L. (1967). *Organisational Behaviour and Human Performance, 2,* 122-142.

Odden, A., & Busch, C. (1998). *Funding schools for high performance management: Strategies for improving the use of school resources.* San Francisco: Jossey-Bass.

Rossett, A. (1999). *First things fast: A handbook for performance analysis.* San Francisco: Jossey-Bass Pfeiffer.

Stufflebeam, D., Madaus, G., & Kellaghan, T. (Eds.). (2000). *Evaluation models: Viewpoints on educational and human services evaluation* (2nd ed.). Boston: Kluwer.

U.S. Department of Education. (2001). *The Elementary & Secondary Education Act as reauthorized by the No Child Left Behind Act.* Washington, DC: Author.

Worthen, B., Sanders, J., & Fitzpatrick, J. (1997). *Program evaluation: Alternative approaches and practical guidelines* (2nd ed.). New York: Longman.

Leping Liu
D. LaMont Johnson

Web-Based Resources and Applications: Quality and Influence

SUMMARY. This paper evaluates the quality of two major types of Web resources for K-12 education–information for research, and interactive applications for teaching and learning. It discusses an evaluation on the quality of 1,025 pieces of Web information (articles, research reports, news, and statistics) and 900 Web applications (tutorials, drills, games, and tests) used by K-12 teachers and students over a six-year period from 1998 to 2004. Findings suggest that (a) quality differs among information from different Web domains (.com, .org, .edu, and .gov); (b) quality differs among applications by different designers (professional designers, college students, K-12 teachers, and university professors); and (c) the quality of a Web-based learning application influences a student's using and learning with it. Challenges and potentials of using the two types of Web resources to improve learning are discussed. A design-quality model is developed and tested. *[Article copies available for a fee from The Haworth Document Delivery Service: 1-800-HAWORTH. E-mail address: <docdelivery@haworthpress.com> Website: <http://www.HaworthPress.com> © 2004 by The Haworth Press, Inc. All rights reserved.]*

LEPING LIU is Associate Professor, Department of Counseling and Educational Psychology, College of Education, University of Nevada, Reno, Reno, NV 89557 (E-mail: liu@unr.edu).

D. LAMONT JOHNSON is Professor, Department of Counseling and Educational Psychology, College of Education, University of Nevada, Reno, Reno, NV 89557 (E-mail: ljohnson@unr.edu).

[Haworth co-indexing entry note]: "Web-Based Resources and Applications: Quality and Influence." Liu, Leping, and D. LaMont Johnson. Co-published simultaneously in *Computers in the Schools* (The Haworth Press, Inc.) Vol. 21, No. 3/4, 2004, pp. 131-147; and: *Web-Based Learning in K-12 Classrooms: Opportunities and Challenges* (ed: Jay Blanchard, and James Marshall) The Haworth Press, Inc., 2004, pp. 131-147. Single or multiple copies of this article are available for a fee from The Haworth Document Delivery Service [1-800-HAWORTH, 9:00 a.m. - 5:00 p.m. (EST). E-mail address: docdelivery@haworthpress.com].

Digital Object Identifier: 10.1300/J025v21n03_13

KEYWORDS. Web-based resources, Web-based learning applications, quality model, quality evaluation

The World Wide Web has been a central resource for teaching and learning (Aviv & Golan, 1998; Barnard, 1997; Berge, 1997; Coombs & Rodd, 2001) in a variety of subject areas over the past two decades (Cunningham & Billingsley, 2003; Lever-Duffy, McDonald & Mizell, 2005; Maddux, Ewing-Taylor & Johnson, 2002). In the literature, two major types of widely used Web resources in education were apparent: (a) information for research, such as articles, research reports, news, or statistics; and (b) interactive learning applications, such as tutorials, drills, games, or video products which were developed and posted on the Web by other educators or designers (Brem, Russell & Weems, 2001; Lever-Duffy, McDonald & Mizell, 2005; Liu, 2001; Murphy, 2004; Shelly, Cashman, Gunter & Gunter, 2003; Tsai & Tsai, 2003). With the rapid development of the Internet, it is hard for one to imagine or even estimate the number of resources available on the Web today. For example, our Google search for "science game" resulted in 4,250,000 links; and, from a random exploration of ten links, we found an average of 45 online science games.

Unfortunately, no evidence showed significant impact of using Web resources on student learning (Maddux, Ewing-Taylor & Johnson, 2002; Torgerson & Elbourne, 2002). In an analysis of 102 technology integration case studies, Johnson and Liu (2000) found that using Web resources and activities did not contribute to either the success of technology integration or student learning.

Researchers have identified three factors that contribute to effectively using Web resources: (a) quality of information, (b) design of the learning applications, and (c) strategies of integration (Boer & Collis, 2001; Brem, Russell & Weems, 2001; Liu & Cheeks, 2001; Owston, 2000; Shackelford, 1999). These same three factors later were found to influence student attitudes toward using, and learning with, Web resources. Furthermore, the quality of the information and the design of an application also influence the quality of teaching and learning, the successful integration of technology, and the effective use of Web resources (Liu & Johnson, 1998; Liu & Velasquez-Bryant, 2003).

The purpose of this study was to provide an overall picture of the main quality attributes of K-12 Web resources, their influence on student learning, and the role of instructional design in technology integration.

This paper includes three parts. In Part One, we discuss a previous study (Liu, 2000) that examined 1,025 pieces of K-12 research information (articles, research reports, news, and statistics) from different Web domains (.com, .org, .edu, and .gov), in terms of five major quality attributes: accuracy, authority, coverage, currency, and verifiability. In Part Two, we discuss the examination of 180 Web applications (tutorials, drills, games, and tests) by different designers (professional designers, college students, K-12 teachers, and university professors), in terms of four design attributes: *Quality of Information, Design of Information, Quality of Technology Use*, and *Design of Technology Use*. Finally, in Part Three, we discuss the results of an analysis of 900 Web applications, the influence of the applications on student learning, and a prediction model.

PART ONE:
QUALITY OF WEB INFORMATION FOR K-12 RESEARCH

When K-12 teachers and students search the Web for research information, they usually browse four types of Web domains: .com, .edu, .org, and .gov. Frequently, the Web information provides useful data to answer their research questions, but it is probable that not all the information is accurate, unbiased, reputable, scientifically valid, or up to date (Leshin, 1998). How could teachers and students base their research on such tenuous information? To select high-quality information, teachers and students need to critically evaluate the information.

From a collection of research references (Liu, 2000) found on the Web by 130 pre-service students enrolled in an introductory college-level course, *Using Information Effectively in Education*, we randomly selected 1,025 pieces of information to evaluate. This research information included articles, research reports, news, or statistics from four Web domains (.com, .org, .edu, and .gov) and focused on educational issues at that time (1998-2001). It was evaluated on five quality attributes (accuracy, authority, coverage, currency, and verifiability) using a checklist (see Appendix A). Findings (see Figure 1) indicate that:

1. information from .edu Web sites ranked highest on *accuracy* and *coverage*,
2. information from .gov Web sites ranked highest on *authority* and *verifiability*,

3. information from .com Web sites ranked highest on *currency*, and
4. the quality of information from .org Web sites was not as good as the other three in any of the five quality attributes.

It is interesting to note that none of the information from the four Web domains perfectly met all five quality criteria. This indicates a challenge to educators seeking appropriate Web information for research or teaching.

PART TWO:
QUALITY OF WEB-BASED LEARNING APPLICATIONS

Web-Based Learning Applications

The term *Web-based learning application* can be defined as instructional content or activity delivered through the Web that (a) teaches a

FIGURE 1. Qualities of Web information by domains.

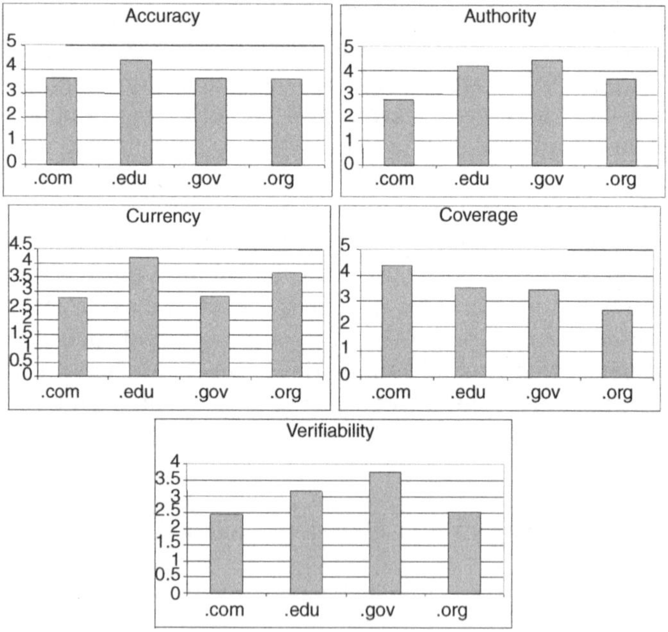

focused concept, (b) meets specific learning objectives, (c) provides a learner-centered context, and (d) is an individual and reusable piece (Barker, Winterstein & Wright, 2004; Dodero, Aedo & Diaz, 2002; Murphy, 2004).

Web-based learning applications can be categorized into two formats: (a) hypertext format–those developed with HTML or other hypertext editors–such as WebQuests, online lecture notes, reading materials, or other instructional materials; and (b) hypermedia format–those developed directly with scripting language (e.g., HTML, DHTML, XHTML, or JAVA) and incorporating such multimedia products as graphics, animations, video or audio clips; and also those initially developed with multimedia authoring software (e.g., *Flash*, *Director*, *Authorware*, *ToolBook*, or *HyperStudio*), and converted to a Web-run version, then published on the Internet, such as online games, drills, tests, or video products.

Web-based learning applications are designed to provide information and interactions. Most hypertext applications are designed to provide content information or guidelines to learning activities. Dynamic online activities, those multimedia instructional programs are designed to carry out interaction, enable users to learn the content or perform the activities by interacting with the learning application directly from the Web. More and more online learning applications tend to have both functions.

Variables Related to the Quality of an Application

To evaluate the quality of Web-based applications, four variables were derived from a technology integration model (Liu & Velasquez-Bryant, 2003) and used to measure the design quality: (a) *Quality of Information*–evaluates content quality (e.g., accuracy, clarity, currency, or verifiability); (b) *Design of Information*–measures the extent to which instructional design components (e.g., audience analysis, content analysis, assignment design and delivery, assessment implementation) are integrated into the content; (c) *Quality of Technology Use*–measures the quality of technology applied to the learning application (e.g., the screen design, orientation, navigation, or interaction); and (d) *Design of Technology Use*–examines the extent to which instructional design principles are integrated into the technology (e.g., the match between content information and the media use or delivery methods, or the match between the required technology skill and the grade level of the targeted audience).

Another factor related to the quality of a Web-based application is the designer of the application. Most applications used in K-12 classroom are developed by either professional designers, college students, school teachers, or university professors. With different professional backgrounds, these designers tend to have different design emphases. One purpose of the current study therefore was to investigate whether or how Web-based applications by different designers differ in quality.

Research Question

The purpose of this particular study was to answer the question:

> Are there significant mean differences in the quality of Web-based learning applications (as measured by the four design-related variables: *Quality of Information*, *Design of Information*, *Quality of Technology Use*, and *Design of Technology Use*) that were created by different designers (professional designers, college students, school teachers, and university professors)?

Sampling

From 900 pre-determined Web-based learning applications (see the sampling in Part Three), four equal-sized random groups of applications were selected. Each group contained 45 applications designed by one of the four types of designers correspondingly: professional designers, college students, school teachers, and university professors. The sum of the four groups, a total of 180 applications, formulated the sample to examine the research question.

This sample of 180 applications covered the subject areas of arithmetic, algebra, geometry, reading, writing, science, Spanish, history, geography, and social science; and consisted of WebQuests, instructional materials, drills, games, tests, and instructional video clips.

Instruments and Measurements

A Likert-style instrument (Appendix B) was used to measure the four quality-variables: *Quality of Information*, *Design of Information*, *Quality of Technology Use*, and *Design of Technology Use*. This instrument consisted of 32 positive statements sorted into four categories with eight statements in each category. The eight statements in each category measured one quality variable. Each statement was scored from 1 (strongly disagree) to 5 (strongly agree). The score for each variable was the sum of eight statements, and the highest possible score was 40. Higher scores represented better quality of learning applications. The reliability coefficient alpha for this instrument was 0.826.

Data Analysis and Results

According to the research question, multivariate analysis of variance was conducted, in which the dependent variable (DV) was the combined *Quality of Design*, as measured by *Quality of Information* (DV$_1$), *Design of Information* (DV$_2$), *Quality of Technology Use* (DV$_3$), and *Design of Technology Use* (DV$_4$). The independent variable (IV) was *Designer* at four levels–professional designers, college students, K-12 teachers, and university professors. The results from the data analysis follow.

First, the Box's Test was significant ($F_{(30, 86165)} = 2.299, p = 0.001$), indicating that the assumption of equal variances is violated. Therefore, instead of using the Wilks' Lambda test, Pillai's Trace test was used (Mertler & Vannatta, 2002, p. 126). MANOVA results show that significant differences were found among the designer categories on the dependent variables: Pillai's Trace value was 0.465 ($F_{(12, 525)} = 8.018, p < 0.0001, \eta^2 = 0.155$).

A univariate ANOVA was conducted as the follow-up test. ANOVA results indicate that the *Quality of Information* significantly differs for designers ($F_{(3, 176)} = 4.478, p < 0.005, \eta^2 = 0.071$); *Design of Information* significantly differs for designers ($F_{(3, 176)} = 6.918, p < 0.0001, \eta^2 = 0.105$); *Quality of Technology Use* significantly differs for designers ($F_{(3,176)} = 14.954, p < 0.0001, \eta^2 = 0.203$); and *Design of Technology Use* significantly differs for designers ($F_{(3, 176)} = 3.071, p < 0.009, \eta^2 = 0.050$).

Results from the post hoc test show the differences (see Figure 2): (a) applications designed by K-12 teachers ($p < 0.01$) and university professors ($p < 0.01$) had higher scores on the *Quality of Information* than those by professional designers; (b) applications designed by college students ($p < 0.027$), K-12 teachers ($p < 0.0001$) and university professors ($p < 0.0001$) had higher scores on the *Design of Information* than those by professional designers; (c) applications designed by professional designers ($p < 0.001$) and university professors ($p < 0.002$) had higher scores on the Quality of Technology Use than those by K-12 teachers; and (d) applications designed by university professors ($p < 0.023$) had higher scores on the *Design of Technology Use* than those by professional designers.

Figure 2 illustrates the mean scores on each dependent variable by designers. The results detail the quality differences among applications created by different designers.

PART THREE: INFLUENCE ON STUDENT LEARNING

Knowing the strengths and weaknesses of Web-based applications by different designers enable educators to take advantage of those strengths and make adjustments to counteract weaknesses. The extent to which they understand the quality of an application would subsequently influence their design of a lesson or learning activity and, hence, student learning. The purpose of Part Three of this study was to show the relationship between the quality variables and student use and learning of Web-based applications.

FIGURE 2. Quality of Web-based applications by developers.

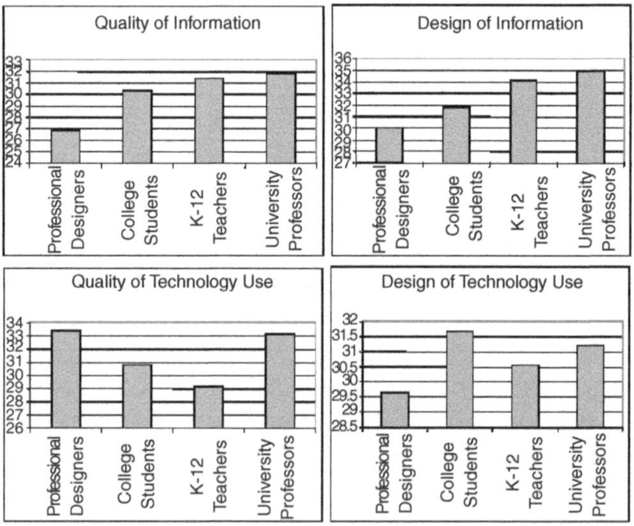

Research Questions

The research question examined in Part Three is:

> Can student learning be predicted by any of the four quality variables (*Quality of Information, Design of Information, Quality of Technology Use*, and *Design of Technology Use*)?

Sample

The sample used to answer this research question was 900 online K-12 learning applications that covered the subject areas of arithmetic, algebra, geometry, reading, writing, science, Spanish, history, geography, and social science; and consisted of WebQuests, instructional materials, drills, games, tests, and instructional video clips.

Of the 900 online learning applications, 375 were selected by 75 teacher education students, from six classes of an introductory technology integration course, in a western U.S. university from 2002 to 2004. The other 525 applications were selected by 105 teacher education students, from four classes of an introductory technology course and four classes of a design course, in an eastern U.S. university from 1999 to 2002.

Procedure

All 180 students (75 plus 105) completed a technology integration project in which each student (referred to as a *mentor*) worked with a K-12 student (referred to as a *protégé*) to design and complete five learning tasks using five Web-based applications. First each mentor determined five learning objectives for the protégé, and evaluated and selected five K-12 online learning applications that met the learning objectives. The mentor subsequently developed lesson plans and five learner-centered activities for the five online applications.

Following the lesson plan, the protégé interacted with the five online applications, performed five activities, and completed the assigned learning tasks. Simultaneously, the mentor observed and scored the protégé's performance based on four criteria: (a) completion of the Web applications, (b) completion of the learning tasks, (c) solving a similar problem, and (d) solving a relevant problem.

By the conclusion of the technology integration project, each mentor had evaluated five online applications, and observed the protégé's performance on five learning activities. Therefore, he/she had collected 10 sets of data: 5 sets of quality evaluation scores on the Web-based applications, and 5 sets of performance observation scores on student learning.

Instruments and Measurements

The instrument used in Part Two (Appendix B) was used to evaluate the Web-based applications; again, the maximum score for each quality variable was 40.

Student learning was measured by the four observation criteria described previously. Each criterion was scored from 1 to 5. The score for each learning activity was the sum of four criteria scores and the highest possible score was 20. Higher scores represented better performance.

Data Analysis I: Generating the Model

Data analysis was performed in two steps. In the first step, the *western data* (data from the western state university, $N = 375$) were used to perform multiple regression analyses and generate a prediction model. The four design-related variables (*Quality of Information, Design of Information, Quality of Technology Use,* and *Design of Technology Use*) were treated as predictor variables, and student *Learning Performance* was the response variable. The results follow.

The linear regression trend was significant ($F_{(4, 374)} = 159.064$, $p < 0.0001$), indicating that the linear model was the desired model that represented the data better than other regression models. Next, the t statistic for each predictor variable was examined: *Quality of Information* ($t = 2.227$, $p < 0.027$), *Design of Information* ($t = 5.719$, $p < 0.0001$), *Quality of Technology Use* ($t = 2.036$, $p < 0.042$), and *Design of Technology Use* ($t = 6.943$, $p < 0.0001$). The t statistics for four quality variables were all significant, indicating that all four variables significantly contributed to the variation of the response variable *Learning Performance*. R-square of the model (R^2) was 0.632, suggesting that approximately 63% of the variation of the response variable *Learning Performance* could be explained by this model, or by the variation in the four quality variables.

The regression analysis generated a set of coefficients that were used to formulate the regression equation:

Learning $= -3.786 + 0.061(QI) + 0.058(DI) + 0.217(QT) + 0.249(DT)$

According to this equation, a one-unit increase in DT (score for the variable *Design of Technology Use*), for example, would increase 0.249 units on the *Learning Performance* score.

Data Analysis II: Testing the Model

In the second step, the *eastern data* (data from the eastern U.S. university, $N = 525$) were used to test the prediction model. We wanted to see whether the prediction model and the relationships developed from the *western data* could be used to predict the relationships in the *eastern data*.

To test the model, first we calculated the predicted values of *Learning Performance* using the regression equation (generated from the *western data*) with the raw data in the *eastern data*. The procedures of calculating the predicted values can be found in Appendix C.

Secondly, we tested the model (expressed in the regression equation) by examining whether there was any difference between the predicted values and the original observed values of the variable *Learning Performance*. If there was no difference, this model developed from the *western data* had successfully predicted the relationships in the *eastern data*.

Paired t tests were conducted, and the results indicate that there was no difference between the predicted values and the observed values for the variable *Learning Performance* ($t_{(524)} = 0.040$, $p < 0.968$), indicating that this model could reliably predict the relationships between the quality of online application design and how students use and learn with the application.

CONCLUSIONS

In summary, in our examination of the quality of Web information and Web-based learning applications, we found (a) quality differs among information from different Web domains (.com, .org, .edu, and .gov); and (b) quality differs among applications by different designers (professional designers, college students, K-12 teachers, and university professors). We also found that the four quality variables (*Quality of Information*, *Design of Information*, *Quality of Technology Use*, and *Design of Technology Use*) were linearly related to student learning, and the prediction model was found reliable in predicting the same relationships. Data examined in this study were collected over the past six years from two different areas of the United States, which we believe should reflect the common issues in the field. Furthermore, the findings from the current study have revealed the following challenges to educators.

Challenge One

Since Web information from different sources and applications by different designers all have strengths and weaknesses, when a teacher selects information or applications from the Web, he/she may be confronted with a dilemma: What should I or shouldn't I use? The challenge is to employ instructional design principles to analyze the information or application, and to develop a set of learning procedures that will take advantage of the strengths and make adjustments to counteract the weaknesses of the application. Although, the basic instructional design principles are the same, specific plans or strategies are always needed when using specific Web applications.

Challenge Two

Most existing Web-based learning applications were developed by educators for their own teaching/learning purposes (Cunningham & Billingsley, 2003; Lever-Duffy, McDonald & Mizell, 2005), and therefore may not be adaptable for other teaching/learning purposes. The challenge, then, is that teachers may want (and need) to design their own Web-based learning application to target specific purposes and objectives. However, technically, economically, and politically, this may be a difficult undertaking.

Challenge Three

We have found a lack of fit between what exists on the Web and what we as educators and students need. The existing applications may not be consistent with our national standards–the curriculum standards for each subject area, and technology standards for teachers, or for students at different grade levels. Our teachers and students need more standards-based applications on the Web. The challenge is for Web application producers to establish a connection between their design and educational standards.

Challenge Four

Looking back at the history of using the Web in education, it started with using Web information for research, moved to using interactive applications for learning, and finally to using the Web as a communication tool. What will our future use be? The challenge is to prepare educators and students for the future. More and more new Web products will be available for education (Barker, Winterstein & Wright, 2004; Dodero, Aedo & Diaz, 2002; Jafari, 2002; Murphy, 2004). With any new application, quality is still an issue, as well as integration and instructional design.

In this paper, we have described the development of a quality model and the relationship among design variables, quality variables, and student learning. It is our hope that these results may be used, or even re-examined again, by other educators and researchers for current and future Web-based applications.

REFERENCES

Aviv, R., & Golan, G. (1998). Pedagogic communication patterns in collaborative telelearning. *Journal of Education Technology Systems, 26*(3), 201-201.

Barker, S., Winterstein, A. P., & Wright, K. E. (2004). Tools for creating e-learning: Learning objects. *Athletic Therapy Today, 9*(1), 10-15.

Barnard, J. (1997). The World Wide Web and higher education: The promise of virtual universities and online libraries. *Educational Technology, 37*(3), 30-35.

Berge, Z. (1997). Computer conferencing and the on-line classroom. *International Journal of Educational Telecommunications, 3*(1), 3-21.

Boer, W. D., & Collis, B. (2001). Implementation and adaptation experiences with a WWW-based course management system. *Computer in the Schools, 17*(3/4), 127-146.

Brem, S. K., Russell, J., & Weems, L. (2001). Science on the Web: Student evaluations of scientific arguments. *Discourse Processes, 32*(2/3), 191-213.

Coombs, S. J., & Rodd, J. (2001). Using the Internet to deliver higher education: A cautionary tale about achieving good practice. *Computers in the Schools, 17*(3/4), 67-90.

Cunningham, C. A., & Billingsley, M. (2003). *Curriculum Webs.* New York, NY: Allyn & Bacon.

Dodero, J. M., Aedo, I., & Diaz, P. (2002). Participative knowledge production of learning objects for e-books. *The Electronic Library, 20*(4), 296-305.

Jafari, A. (2002). Conceptualizing intelligent agents for teaching and learning. *Educause Quarterly,* No. 3, 28-34.

Johnson, D. L., & Liu, L. (2000). First steps toward a statistically generated information technology integration model. *Computers in the Schools, 16*(2), 3-12.

Leshin, C. B. (1998). *Internet adventures: Integrating the Internet into the curriculum.* Needham Heights, MA: Allyn & Bacon.

Lever-Duffy, J., McDonald, J. B., & Mizell, A. P. (2005). *Teaching and learning with technology.* New York: Allyn & Bacon.

Liu, L. (2001). On-line delivery of multimedia courseware: Issues and effects. In J. D. Price, D. A. Willis, N. Davis, & J. Willis (Eds.), *Technology & Teacher Education Annual 2001* (pp. 1126-1131). Charlottesville, VA: AACE.

Liu, L. (2000, October). Critically evaluating the quality of Web information. Presentation at MAEUC (*Maryland Association for the Educational Uses of Computers*) Forum 2000, Towson, MD.

Liu, L., & Cheecks, C. (2001). Assessing technology-assisted use of information. In J. D. Price, D. A. Willis, N. Davis, & J. Willis (Eds.), Technology & Teacher Education Annual 2001 (pp. 2374-2377). Charlottesville, VA: AACE.

Liu, L., & Johnson, L. (1998). A computer achievement model: Computer attitude and computer achievement. *Computers in the Schools, 14*(3/4), 33-54.

Liu, L., & Velasquez-Bryant, N. J. (2003). An information technology integration system and its life cycle: What is missing? *Computers in the Schools, 20*(1/2), pp. 93-106.

Maddux, C. D., Ewing-Taylor, J., & Johnson, D. L. (2002). The light and dark sides of distance education. *Computers in the Schools, 19*(3/4), 1-7.

Mertler, C. A., & Vannatta, R. A. (2002). *Advanced and multivariate statistical methods: Practical application and interpretation* (2nd ed.). Los Angeles, CA: Pyrczak Publishing.

Murphy, E. (2004). Moving from theory to practice in the design of Web-based learning using a learning object approach. *E-Journal of Instructional Science and Technology, 7*(1). Retrieved March 10, 2004, from http://www.usq.edu.edu/electpub/e-jist/

Owston, R. D. (2000). Evaluating Web-based learning environments: Strategies and insights. *CyberPsychology and Behavior, 3*(1), 79-87.

Shackelford, J. (1999). Assessing the strengths and limits of websites: The Web form in action. *Feminist Economics, 5*(1), 78-90.

Shelly, G. B., Cashman, T. J., Gunter, R. E., & Gunter, G. A. (2003). *Teacher discovering computers: Integrating technology in the classroom* (3rd ed.). Boston, MA: Course Technology.

Torgerson, C. J., & Elbourne, D. (2002). A systematic review and meta-analysis of the effectiveness of information and communication technology on the teaching of spelling. *Journal of Research in Reading, 25*(2), 129-143.

Tsai, M. J., & Tsai, C. C. (2003). Information searching strategies in Web-based science learning: The role of Internet self-efficacy. *Innovations in Education and Teaching International, 40*(1), 43-50.

APPENDIX A
Web Information Evaluation

Accuracy

1. Is the material free from error?
2. Does the information come from a published document, such as a research paper or report, historical document, news publications?
3. Does the document include a bibliography and sufficient references?
4. Are there any editors or reviewers?
5. How reputable is the publisher?

Authority

6. Who is responsible for the site?
7. Is the author's name clearly visible? Is there a link to the author's home page or e-mail address?
8. What are the author's qualifications on the subject?
9. Does the author have credentials to be an expert on the topic? (educational background, experiences)
10. Have you ever encountered the author's name in your reading or in bibliographies?

Currency

11. Is the topic/content of the work up to date?
12. Are current issues under the topic included?
13. Are the bibliographies up to date?
14. Is the publication date of the information clearly labeled?
15. When was the site last updated?

Coverage

16. Is the topic clearly defined?
17. Are related topics or issues included?
18. Are the topics included explored in depth?
19. Are the topics included supported by efficient literature?
20. Is background information on the topics included?

Verifiability

21. Can the data be verified?
22. Does it appear to be well-researched?
23. Does the author make generalizations without proof or validation?
24. Does the data have statistical validity?
25. Is it primary information or secondary information?

APPENDIX B
Evaluation Criteria for Web-Based Learning Applications

Information

1. Language is accurate.
2. Language is easy to understand.
3. Language is error free
4. Language and materials are at the identified grade level.
5. Resources are sufficient.
6. Resources are updated.
7. Materials and resources are verifiable.
8. Designer's information is included.

Design of Information

9. Activity goals/objectives are clearly presented.
10. Task and processes are designed to achieve the goals/objectives.
11. Task and processes are designed for learners at the identified grade level.
12. Higher level thinking is engaged.
13. Processes are designed in a learner-oriented approach.
14. Resources are closely related to the task/activities
15. Assignments/exercise requirements reflect the knowledge/skills that match objectives.
16. Evaluation criteria match the activity processes and objectives.

Technology

17. Screen layout is balanced, and graphics are positioned appropriately.
18. It is easy to find where you are in the program.
19. It is easy to find where you want to go within the program.
20. Users can stop and find a way to exit when they need to.
21. All resource links work well.
22. Help or assistance instructions are provided and easy to access.
23. Instruction materials can be downloaded or printed out in a clear layout.
24. Interactions between user and the program are user-friendly.

Design of Technology Use

25. Web is appropriate for performing this activity.
26. Technology skills needed for the activity match learners' developmental level.

27. Interface design is appropriate to the grade level and the topic/subject area.
28. Organization of resource links matches the activity processes.
29. Use of multimedia matches the objectives of the activity.
30. Design approach (linear or non-linear) matches task processes and objectives.
31. The interactions are designed to meet the learning objectives.
32. Mapping of the contents and activities is available.

APPENDIX C
Procedures of Calculating the Predicted Values

1. Opening the *eastern data* file from Excel;
2. Creating a new column named "predicted values" right after the column that coded the original raw scores of *Learning Performance;*
3. Adding a calculation function on to this new column according to regression equation: Learning Performance = $-3.786 + 0.061(QI) + 0.058(DI) + 0.217(QT) + 0.249(DT)$;
4. In the calculation function, exact column names for the four predictor variables (QI, DI, QT, and DT) were used correspondingly. For example, in the datasheet, if the four variables were in columns C, D, E, and F, then the function added into the first cell of the new column should be " $= -3.786 + 0.061*C1 + 0.058*D1 + 0.217*E1 + 0.249*F1$";
5. Copying this function onto all the cells in the new column. All the calculated values then appeared in this new column, which were the predicted *Learning Performance* scores.

Cleborne D. Maddux

The Web in K-12 Education:
Is There a Future?

SUMMARY. Growth in size and popularity of the Web over the last 10 years has been remarkable. There are now many calls to make the Web the center of K-12 schooling. However, there are many problems that must be solved before the Web can be fully integrated into curricula in public schools. Such problems can be categorized as practical or pedagogical in nature. Pedagogical problems include those barriers to Web integration that are caused by the nature of the education subculture and the culture at large. These are the most difficult problems to solve and would call for a nation-wide commitment to true individualized education. *[Article copies available for a fee from The Haworth Document Delivery Service: 1-800-HAWORTH. E-mail address: <docdelivery@haworthpress.com> Website: <http://www.HaworthPress. com> © 2004 by The Haworth Press, Inc. All rights reserved.]*

KEYWORDS. Web integration, individualized education, barriers to Web use in schools

Popular and professional literature, the media, and the Web itself have lately been replete with articles singing the praises of the World

CLEBORNE D. MADDUX is Associate Editor for Research, *Computers in the Schools*, and Foundation Professor, Department of Counseling and Educational Psychology, University of Nevada, Reno, Reno, NV 89557 (E-mail: maddux@unr.edu).

[Haworth co-indexing entry note]: "The Web in K-12 Education: Is There a Future?" Maddux, Cleborne D. Co-published simultaneously in *Computers in the Schools* (The Haworth Press, Inc.) Vol. 21, No. 3/4, 2004, pp. 149-165; and: *Web-Based Learning in K-12 Classrooms: Opportunities and Challenges* (ed: Jay Blanchard, and James Marshall) The Haworth Press, Inc., 2004, pp. 149-165. Single or multiple copies of this article are available for a fee from The Haworth Document Delivery Service [1-800-HAWORTH, 9:00 a.m. - 5:00 p.m. (EST). E-mail address: docdelivery@haworthpress.com].

http://www.haworthpress.com/web/CITS
© 2004 by The Haworth Press, Inc. All rights reserved.
Digital Object Identifier: 10.1300/J025v21n03_14

Wide Web as a revolutionary new tool in education. One index of the magnitude of the interest in the use of the Web in education is that a recent search with a popular search engine (*Google*, at http://www. google.com) produced nearly 12 million sites including both the term "Web" and "education."

In light of the incredible proliferation of books and articles dealing with the topic, the question in the title of the present article at first glance seems hardly worth asking, since the answer to it appears to be self-evident. Indeed, the title was chosen as a tongue-in-cheek device to draw attention and stimulate interest by posing a question that many, if not most, educators and members of the general public assume involves a forgone conclusion in the affirmative.

Taken at face value, the title *is* ludicrous. It is clearly inevitable that the Web will have a place in the future of K-12 education. Why? Because the Web has attained such a level of cultural momentum that it is unlikely that any individuals or groups could prevent that future presence, even if they tried to do so. After all, computers and the Web have become ubiquitous, and have had a profound, worldwide impact on practically every aspect of modern life.

One indication of the sweeping influence of the Web is its phenomenal growth in both size and popularity. When President Clinton took office for his first term as U.S. President, there were only about 50 pages on the Web. When he left office, the Web had grown to at least a billion pages. Although no one knows the exact size of the Web today, Sullivan (2003) reports that by August of 2003, there were at least 3.3 billion pages on the Web, and over 600 million users worldwide. Then too, the Web has become a major source of news and other information, and has been shown to compete with television as an entertainment medium in the United States and Canada, where more time was spent surfing the Web in one recent three-month period than the combined playback time of all rented videotapes in those two countries (Masotto, 1995).

So, the Web *will* have a place in the future of K-12 education–its place in the worldwide culture at large is too prominent for it to be otherwise. Thus, the title of the present article asks a question to which we all already know the answer. However, there is another critical, unstated, but clearly implied, question, and one with an answer that is decidedly not self-evident. We should not ask whether the Web will merely be present in classrooms of the future, *but whether it will fulfill its considerable, and much-lauded potential to revolutionize teaching and learning for the better.*

As previously stated, I feel sure that teachers and students of the future will have access of some kind to the World Wide Web. I am far less sure that the access they will enjoy will help bring about fundamental, important improvements in teaching or learning in K-12 schools.

This paper will explore some of the issues and problems in integrating the Web into teaching and learning in K-12 education, and will attempt to come to some reasonable conclusions about the likely result of Web use in K-12 schools of the future.

STRUCTURING A DISCUSSION OF THE WEB IN K-12 EDUCATION

The topic is so large, with so many nuances, that finding a logical starting place is a daunting task. There are undoubtedly many ways to structure a discussion on the present and future role of the Web in K-12 education. Although admittedly mundane, a discussion of claimed advantages including disadvantages or barriers may be the most efficient approach.

Claimed Advantages of Integrating the Web into Education

There is no shortage of professional and popular literature espousing the benefits of Web use in education. Owston (1997) summed up this state of affairs when he suggested that "nothing before has captured the imagination and interest of educators simultaneously around the globe more than the World Wide Web" (p. 27). Advocates of Web use in education are citing many different types of advantages. Perhaps the most common of these are advantages that might be categorized as *practical* in nature.

Practical Advantages

Can the Web Improve Access to Education?

One of the most commonly cited reasons for supporting Web use in education is that the Web can greatly increase access to education. The argument is that the Web can make education accessible to students who are unable or unwilling to come to a traditional campus and attend face-to-face classes. This inability to attend may be due to many different student factors such as residence in remote geographical locations, religious/philosophical objections of parents to perceived values taught in public schools, need to work during the school day, disciplinary problems or problems with the law, medical problems, disability, etc.

Owston (1997) discussed the potential of the Web to improve access to education and concluded that, while increased access to this point has primarily been in bringing higher education opportunities to students who are unable to come to campus, there are three aspects of K-12 education in which the Web has already improved access and that is destined to become even more important in the future. These aspects include (a) *home schooling*, (b) *alternative schooling*, and (c) *extension course delivery*.

With regard to home schooling, Owston (1997) suggests that the Web has increased access to high-quality teaching and learning materials and has the potential to provide increased interaction with peers. This is important, since these are the two areas most often cited as weaknesses of home schooling.

It is significant also because of the growing number of children who are being home schooled. Lines (1995) examined data gathered in 1990 from state education agencies, distributors of popular curricular packages, and home schooling organizations. She then assumed modest growth and estimated that by 1995, at least half a million children, or one percent of all school-age students in the country, were being home schooled. Baumann (2002), in a much more rigorous study, used the 1994 October Current Population Survey (CPS) (U.S. Census Bureau, 2000) and the National Household Education Surveys (NHES) of 1999 to estimate the extent of home schooling. He concluded that the number of children being home schooled had risen to about 790,000 by 1999. Most estimates of the number of children who are presently being educated at home are in excess of one million.

Owston (1997) suggests that alternative schooling and extension course delivery are two other areas that are poised for growth due to the Web. There is no wide agreement on the definition of what constitutes an alternative school (Lange & Sletten 2002), but Paglin and Fager (1997) suggest that such schools are for children who are not succeeding in regular public schools or who are at risk for school failure. The National Center for Education Statistics (Kleiner, Porch, & Farris, 2002) has said that the number of such schools is growing rapidly, and as of October 1, 2000, 612,900 students, or 1.3% of all public school students were enrolled in public alternative schools. This does not include an additional substantial number who attend private alternative schools.

Owston (1997) identifies extension course delivery as the last of the three areas that have already increased access and that is destined for growth in the near future. He suggests that growth potential exists because the Web makes it possible for high school students to take courses not offered by their traditional, face-to-face schools. Additionally, the Web has already begun to deliver courses to help high school students prepare to take standardized exams and to get started early with college courses. Then too, adults are increasingly using the Web to take extension courses to enable them to continue with interrupted high school careers and obtain high school diplomas while remaining employed.

Barriers to Access

Roschelle and Pea (1999) organized a workshop to evaluate the ideas and advantages of Web use in education that had been suggested by Owston (1997). They invited 115 researchers from 62 public and private institutions and organizations. These individuals critically evaluated and discussed each of Owston's suggested advantages.

With regard to access, they concluded that there are important barriers to access other than distance and time, which were the access problems identified by Owston. They pointed out that for high school students to have true access to college courses, for example, the subject matter of such courses cannot simply be pages from college textbooks transferred to computer screen displays. Rather, such subject matter must first be converted to forms consistent with the strengths and weaknesses of the Web itself. That is, Web content must make use of the "visualization, simulation, and modeling capabilities of advanced technology" (p. 23). Additionally, participants pointed out that there are access problems because the current Web is overly dependent on text while young, elementary school students as well as many high school students are not fluent readers. This text dependency also requires fluent typing skills to gain access to meaningful, Web-based communication tools such as chatrooms and bulletin boards. Other access problems cited by the group were the lack of widely accepted and widely followed standards for Web page design to accommodate users with disabilities and the unsuitability of available Web conferencing tools for use in classrooms with 20 to 40 students.

Finally, the group pointed out that there are problems caused by what might be considered *too much* access. These include access to danger; access to too much, disorganized information at often-inappropriate levels of complexity and detail; and too much access to advertising.

Roschelle and Pea (1999) concluded that the Web has many important weaknesses that must be addressed before it can meet Owston's goal of improving access to education for large groups of students.

Although Roschelle and Pea came to this conclusion in 1999, their points seem to remain well taken in 2004. Many instructional pages on the Web are little more than textbook pages converted to digital format. Most Web pages remain overly dependent on text, and are likely to remain so until broadband connections become much more common in schools and in homes than they are today. Standards exist to help ensure access to those with disabilities, but they are seldom adhered to in Web pages. Popular communication tools still require typing ability, and the day when streaming video can be sent and received in most classrooms and most homes seems far in the future. The Web is as dangerous as ever and inappropriate material is at least as common as it has ever been. Web advertising could be said to be out of control, commercial popups are a major source of frustration, and spam is now comprising about half of all e-mail moved on the Web.

Can the Use of the Web Save Money?

Anyone who has been around computers for any length of time tends to smile when this argument is advanced. One of the few things we should have learned by now is that computerizing an activity almost never saves money. Almost the only reason to computerize an activity is to improve the type and quality of information available, not to make the handling of that information more economical. In fact, in the short run, computerizing any activity almost always increases costs, and this most frequently remains true even for the long run.

It is hard to imagine that integrating the Web in education could save anyone money. Two of the three areas in which Owston (1997) envisions improved access to education through Web use–home schooling and participation in extension courses–would almost certainly require students and their families to invest heavily in computers and Internet service for their homes. Alternative schools (indeed, any schools) might require use of the Web only when on campus, but it is hard to imagine how any heavy school reliance on the Web would not result in the need for the same equipment and Internet service at home.

As any public school administrator knows, incorporating computer technology at school is certainly not a money-saving activity. Indeed, public schools across the nation are struggling with the high cost of acquiring and maintaining up-to-date technology. Survey after survey shows that school districts are finding the recurring high costs necessary to prevent obsolescence a near-impossible burden to carry. Public schools are filled with antiquated equipment and equipment in various states of disrepair. Even universities are finding it difficult to acquire, maintain, and replace computer equipment.

Another financial problem for public schools intent on integrating Web use in their curricula is the problem of antiquated wiring. There are two kinds of wiring causing significant cost problems in public schools attempting to make widespread use of the Web: (a) overburdened electrical circuits that cannot bear the load of dozens or hundreds of simultaneously running computers and peripherals, and (b) the absence of Internet wiring in classrooms built long before the Web was a fact of everyday life. Although the problem of Internet cabling can be solved by the use of wireless networks, and the problem of overburdened electrical circuits lessened by the use of laptop computers, both solutions introduce additional significant hardware, software, support, security, and maintenance costs.

An even more significant problem that is sometimes overlooked when first beginning to consider financial needs is the cost of developing, offering, and administering Web-based courses and programs. Saba (1999) estimates that commercial software companies spend on average a half-million dollars to develop each new educational course or to convert regular, text-based educational material for presentation on the Web. Rochelle and Pea (1999) put that cost at about a million dollars per course. Saba (1999) maintains that schools must enroll at least 500 online students in any course before recouping the high cost of Web course development.

Even if Saba's and others' cost estimates prove to be excessive, there is little doubt that Web course development is more, not less expensive than traditional delivery. The literature is full of articles documenting the fact that at least initially, Web courses are more costly than traditional courses, and there is disagreement as to whether or not online education can ever achieve long-term cost-effectiveness in comparison with traditional, face-to-face courses. Therefore, one must ask, Who will be willing to pay these high start-up costs in K-12 education for the Web?

Participants in the Rochelle and Pea (1999) workshop pointed out the ongoing high rate of failure of educational technology businesses serving the K-12 market, and their increasing reluctance to become involved in course development. Therefore, it seems unlikely that we can soon expect a robust, private sector competition in the development of high-quality Web-based courses. Those in K-12 education may therefore be left with little to choose from when selecting Web-based courses for their own use, and most of what is available to them may be courses developed for use in higher education. Such courses may serve the needs of a relatively small number of K-12 students, but will not be appropriate for large numbers of average students at all levels of public schooling.

PEDAGOGICAL ADVANTAGES

Can the Web Improve Learning?

Thousands of studies have been conducted and many more thousands of articles have been written around the question of whether technology can improve learning. Although the debate goes on, consensus among researchers is coalescing around the idea that it is not technology, but pedagogy that is the critical learning variable (Joy & Garcia, 2000). Some of the leading advocates of this view have been Richard Clark (1983, 1985, 1994) and Robert Gagne (1992). In other words, it may not matter what medium is used–the critical variable is the teaching method that is embedded in whatever medium is used to deliver the content.

This is not the place to debate this issue, although it probably bears mentioning that my colleagues and I have argued that certain technology applications may make some powerful teaching methods available and practical that were not available and practical before the availability of that technology. We have called such educational applications *Type II* applications (Maddux, Johnson, & Willis, 2001; Maddux & Johnson, in press). Thus, while the power may indeed lie in the method rather than the medium, the controversy becomes something of a moot point, if in practice, a positive and powerful method is not available without the medium.

However, asking whether technology can improve teaching and learning may be the wrong question to ask, and asking it is reminiscent of an earlier controversy in the field of information technology in education. That controversy swirled around whether learning to program in the Logo computer language could, as Papert (1980) suggested, make formal operational thinking available to children at earlier ages than formerly thought possible. At the time, the question was never satisfactorily answered, nor is it likely ever to be so answered. The conditions Papert identified as necessary for the teaching of Logo to have the hypothesized effect as a cognitive amplifier–a computer for every child, suspension of grading, discovery learning, etc.–were never widely established in public schools, nor or they likely to be widely established in the near future. Furthermore, many of the researchers investigating the question of whether Logo could act as a cognitive amplifier failed to ensure that the children in question learned to program competently in Logo. In many of these studies, it was unclear as to whether they actually learned the language in any deep, important sense. Obviously, a study in which students do not thoroughly learn to program in Logo is not a true test of the effects of learning to program in that language. Thus, Papert's ideas might today fairly be characterized as never having been adequately tested on a large scale.

The same may be true years from now when we look back and ask whether a fair test was ever made of the idea that the Web can improve teaching and learning. Although surveys show that nearly every school now has an Internet connection, one school connection to the Web is of little or no instructional value, particularly if that connection is in the principal's office or behind the desk in the library. What we would need to test the idea of whether the Web can improve learning would be a reasonable number of connected computers located in classrooms–some ratio of connected computers to students that would make it possible to base the entire school day on Web use.

What is the current school ratio of Internet-connected computers to students? If such data exist, I have not been able to find it. Anecdotally, however, many schools I visit have only one connection, often in the principal's office or behind the desk in the library, or in those schools with more connections, all or most are sometimes located in computer labs, where students have access to them for only one period each week or less.

This begs the question of what the minimum ratio of connected computers to students would need to be in order to put into place curricula that depended heavily on the Web. No one knows, but it seems reasonable that such heavy Web use would demand a classroom ratio of at least one Web-connected computer per two or three students, and one could argue convincingly (as Papert did) that *every* student would need a Web-connected computer in order to completely integrate Web use into K-12 education. We are so far from achieving such a ratio that even suggesting it seems almost as outlandish as it did when Papert proposed it in 1980. Yet without a very low ratio of students to Web-connected computers (arguably, one to one), it is difficult to imagine a fundamental change in the way K-12 classrooms function. After all, what are students who are waiting for Web use expected to do while they wait? It seems obvious that such students would be subjected to traditional methods and materials and the Web would not really be the basis of teaching and learning in that school.

Barriers Caused by the Education Subculture and the Culture at Large

This brings us to a pedagogical barrier to Web integration in K-12 schools that is more significant than any of the barriers discussed to this point. This barrier is caused by the very subculture of K-12 education and the idea of schooling that is part of that subculture, and part of the larger culture as well. In current educational literature, in which political correctness seems in full flower, this need for a change in the idea of what constitutes schooling, teaching, and learning is popularly referred to as the need for a paradigm shift.

It is ironic that many of those using this term identify themselves as proponents of *postmodernism*, an informal and ill-defined, yet currently wildly fashionable philosophical approach that sometimes seems little more than solipsism clothed in a combination of philosophical and educational jargon. Postmodernists reject science and the scientific method on the grounds that there exists no objective reality for science to discover. The irony is that the term *paradigm shift* is being widely used by those who would reject science, yet the term itself comes to us from a 1962 book about the nature of science by Thomas Kuhn. In that book, Kuhn posited that the way science progresses is not by gradual accumulation of knowledge and slow change, but by sudden, large conceptual leaps in which one widely accepted intellectual view of the world is displaced by another, quite different world view. A paradigm shift, then, as defined by Kuhn, is a revolutionary leap to a new way for scientists to think about the world.

Although the term *paradigm shift* is widely used in current educational literature, it is almost certainly insufficient as a term to describe the changes needed to eliminate the barrier to Web integration under consideration at this point. That barrier, which is caused *by how we think about teaching and learning*, also includes *what we value about schools and schooling*. Thus, the barrier is much more than merely intellectual in nature, although it certainly is partly that. More substantively, however, it is cultural in nature, with all that implies about attitudes, values, and resistance to change.

The sheer inertia connected to certain aspects of culture such as formal education should not be underestimated. It often is, in fact, substantial, to say the least. This is a point emphasized by George Kneller in a classic volume entitled *Educational Anthropology* (1965). Kneller explained that changes in one area of culture eventually bring about changes in all other aspects, but that such changes do not take place at the same rate. This is the concept of *cultural lag*, which is the phenomenon that some aspects of culture have a tendency to change much more slowly than others. He goes on to suggest that the most obvious example in the United States is that technology changes much more quickly than attitudes and values.

Thus, computer technology has changed much more rapidly than have the educational values and attitudes that are necessary to promote, or even to permit, the changes in schools necessary to fully integrate computers and the World Wide Web into the educational enterprise. Sherry and Hoffman (1997) make reference to this point in a slightly different way. They assert that the Web itself can be viewed as a subculture, and imply that a clash of subcultures is inevitable when the Web is brought into schools:

> [The Web] has all the key elements of a culture, including its own language, symbols, and other meaning-conveying forms. It is not simply something to be tacked on to an existing structure; as another culture, it is bound to threaten some existing conventions and cultural practices. (Conclusions section, ¶ 1)

It is the threat to existing educational conventions and to the values, attitudes, and practices implicit in the subculture of public school educators and educational policymakers that seems to me to constitute the most imposing barrier to Web integration. One can almost not overestimate the magnitude or scope of changes that would be necessary to make the Web the center of public school curricula. These changes cut across every aspect of the educational enterprise. Profound changes would be necessary in curriculum, behavior management, pre-service teacher education, in-service education, assessment, grading, and, most significantly, in the very concepts of what it means to teach and to learn. Indeed, it is difficult to think of any significant school activity that would not need to be fundamentally altered in a revolutionary way. Clearly, such sweeping changes would constitute much more than the relatively simple and comparatively isolated intellectual act of switching paradigms–they would constitute what Papert himself (1980, 1993) called *megachange*.

Why would such dramatic changes be necessary? Consider the current nature of the Web. At present, it can be thought of, at least metaphorically, and perhaps even literally, as a poorly organized, giant, occasionally interactive encyclopedia containing both accurate and inaccurate information about almost any topic imaginable. Wallace (1999) made similar references to the nature of the Web:

> Instead of being carefully designed to help students learn, content on the Web is varied and unpredictable in its design. . . . Issues of authenticity and authority loom large, and Web sites can be complex and confusing or deep and significant. . . . Clearly, there are both positive and negative features of the new space opened up by the Web. (pp. 3-4)

It seems obvious that making educationally productive use of the Web environment of today would demand a style of teaching and learning that is anything but widespread in today's schools. Whether one calls the necessary changes as demanding "discovery learning," "inquiry," or some other popular, jargon-laden term such as *constructivism*, the point is that centering our curricula on a large, disorganized, interactive encyclopedia filled with information that is sometimes sublime but is more often ridiculous is an extremely tall order. To say that it would call for substantive changes on the part of educators, educational policymakers, and learners, is the height of understatement.

Such changes would demand a massive shift in values related to schooling. They would demand a concentrated, all-out, intensive commitment to *individualized education*–a concept to which educators have paid lip service for decades, with little, if any true progress toward widespread realization.

Assuming that policymakers, administrators, and the public at large could be persuaded to support such an effort and make such a commitment (a very tenuous assumption to begin with), and assuming that the substantial hardware, software, and other access problems could be solved, the work needed by individual teachers would be immense, and beyond the capabilities of many. Wallace (1999) made reference to just five of the almost unlimited number of problems teachers would face if they were to make the Web the center of effective instruction:

1. Planning problems. Teachers would need to anticipate content needed for the year, for the unit of study, and for the daily lesson and somehow limit that content and make the amount and type valid, appropriate, and manageable by students at different levels. This can be done by setting up Web sites containing multiple links to relevant content, for example, but however this problem is addressed, the teacher will be required to invest a great deal of time and effort in advance searching.

2. Problems caused by the need to teach unfamiliar content. These problems would come about because students would find and ask questions about content that is not familiar to the teacher. Teachers would, by necessity, have to internalize the notion that they are guides and learn to function as such with material they themselves have not mastered.

3. Problems caused by the need to help students evaluate the quality of information on the Web. These are problems of authenticity, and given the range of validity of content on the Web, they are extensive.

4. Organizational problems. These problems would come about because individual students must be helped to learn "in a classroom teeming with students and technology and operating under pressures of time and curriculum" (p. 14).

5. Problems of assessment and record keeping. These are problems brought about by the need to keep track of each student's progress and to respond to demands by administration, parents, state departments of education, and the culture at large for teacher accountability for learning.

What Is the Future of the Web in Education?

Predicting anything related to technology is fraught with danger. Technology futurists of the past have seldom been correct with any of their prognostications. However, I stated at the beginning of this article that I am not optimistic about the chances of the Web revolutionizing K-12 education in a positive way. The barriers to a shift to true individualized education, only some of which have been identified in this article, are simply too great and too unlikely to be surmounted to engender much optimism on that score.

Even so, I don't consider myself pessimistic about the Web and education. While I do not believe that the World Wide Web, in its present form, is likely to revolutionize K-12 education in a positive way, I do believe that it has the potential to do so, if only the problems discussed in this article as well as many others could be resolved. That potential is unprecedented in my career as an educator. The Web is in its infancy, but I see it as the most likely catalyst for meaningful educational change that has ever graced the educational landscape. Whether or not the political climate or other cultural conditions will permit that potential to be fulfilled is another matter.

To maintain and extend the spirit of optimism with which I began this final section, I can say that I do, for example, see signs that Web content is improving. There are now a number of sites on the Web that I would consider exemplary, and a sign that more and more educators are beginning to sense the tremendous potential of the Web to make available new and better ways of teaching and learning.

One excellent example is an applet for the study of correlation and regression found at http://www.stat.uiuc.edu/courses/stat100//java/guess/PPApplet.html. This page is maintained by the Department of Statistics at the University of Illinois. This interactive page presents a blank scatterplot into which the user may add data points for the X and Y variables by clicking in the body of the plot. After each data point is added, the program instantly recalculates the correlation coefficient and the regression equation. The line of best fit is also instantly relocated after each change in the data. Plots of residuals against the X variable are available as well as a histogram of residuals.

This applet makes it possible for users to experience a number of important concepts about correlation and regression that cannot be experienced any other way. For example, the distorting effect of a single extreme outlier on a correlation coefficient and on the line of best fit can be seen immediately and can be experienced with many different data sets and with correlation coefficients of differing strength and direction–all in just a few minutes. The ability of the computer program to instantly recalculate correlation coefficients and regression equations and relocate the regression line as the data are changed provides a bridge between the visual and mathematical representations of the data that cannot be obtained with hand calculations or static drawings.

This, I believe, is an example of the true potential of the Web to make new and better ways of teaching and learning available.

However, it is possible to make too much of such Web sites. They cannot, for example, teach themselves. The correlation and regression Web site referred to would be of little, if any, value to any learner without some prior instruction regarding correlation and regression, some understanding of visual representations such as scatterplots and histograms, an exposure to residuals, and, most importantly, without some involvement of a teacher.

But, what kind of changes in the fabric of schooling would be required to facilitate the needed kind of teacher involvement across subject areas and grade levels and throughout the land? The makeover, I believe, would require an all-out commitment to individualized education, discovery learning, and inquiry, with all that implies.

I think there will continue to be more and more sites like the correlation and regression site–sites that make new and better ways of teaching available. Thus, I am optimistic that the educational potential of the Web will continue to grow. I am less optimistic that the education subculture of schooling will be changed sufficiently to enable educators to take advantage of this potential on a large scale.

Many writers have drawn attention to the fact that today's public school classrooms are remarkably unchanged from the classrooms of 50, 60, or even 100 years ago. Many, perhaps even most of these writers, were referring to the physical environment of the classroom, which has indeed remained relatively static over the last century. With the exception of style of dress, speech, and architecture, very little about school has changed. However, these are merely the physical trappings of schooling. What is more discouraging is that the underlying subculture of schooling has changed so little, and it is resistance to these more important changes that threatens to put an end to our hopes of using the Web to transform schooling.

I doubt that the culture at large or the education subculture is prepared to endorse the sweeping changes outlined in this paper necessary to fully commit our efforts to individualized education. I hope I am wrong. Obviously, most of the individuals who have contributed to this volume think that it can be done. I hope they are right. I believe technology has the best potential to be a catalyst for positive educational transformation than has any development in modern times. Let us hope I am proved wrong, and we do not squander that potential.

REFERENCES

Bauman, K. J. (2002, May 16). Home schooling in the United States: Trends and characteristics. *Education Policy Analysis Archives, 10*(26). Retrieved May 30, 2004, from http://epaa.asu.edu/epaa/v10n26.html

Clark, R. E. (1983). Reconsidering research on learning from media. *Review of Educational Research, 53*(4), 445-459.

Clark, R. E. (1985). Evidence for confounding in computer based instruction studies: Analyzing the meta-analyses. *Educational Technology Research and Development, 33*(4), 235-262.

Clark, R. E. (1994). Media will never influence learning. *Educational Technology Research and Development, 42*(2), 21-29.

Gagne, R. M., Briggs, L. J., & Wager, W. W. (1992). Principles of instructional design (4th ed.). Orlando, FL: Harcourt, Brace, Jovanovich.

Joy, E. H., & Garcia, F. (2000). Measuring learning effectiveness: A new look at no-significant-difference findings. *Journal of Asynchronous Learning Networks* *4*(1), 33-39.

Hoffman, L. (2001). *Key statistics on public elementary and secondary schools and agencies: School year 1997–98* (NCES 2001–304r). Washington, DC: U.S. Department of Education, National Center for Education Statistics.

Kleiner, B., Porch, R., & Farris, E. (2002). *Public alternative schools and programs for students at risk of education failure: 2000–01* (NCES 2002–004). Washington, DC: U.S. Department of Education, National Center for Education Statistics.

Kneller, G. (1965). *Educational anthropology: An introduction.* New York: John Wiley.

Kuhn, T. S. (1962). *The structure of scientific revolutions* (2nd ed.). Chicago, IL: The University of Chicago Press.

Lange, C. M., & Sletten, S. J. (2002). *Alternative education: A brief history and research synthesis.* Alexandria, VA: National Association of State Directors of Special Education.

Lines, P.M. (1995). *Home schooling* (ERIC Digest Number 95). Eugene, OR: ERIC Clearinghouse on Educational Management. (ERIC Document Reproduction Service No. ED381849)

Maddux, C. D., & Johnson, D. L. (in press). Type II applications of technology in education. *Computers in the Schools.*

Maddux, C. D., Johnson, D. L., & Willis, J. W. (2001). *Educational computing: Learning with tomorrow's technologies* (3rd. ed.). Boston: Allyn & Bacon.

Masotto, T. (1995). The CommerceNet/Nielsen Internet demographics survey executive summary. Retrieved October 20, 1998, from http://www.commerce.net/work/pilot/nielsen_96/exec_95.html

Nolin, M. J., Montaquila, J., Lennon, J., Kleiner, B., Kim, K., Chapman, C., Chandler, K., Creighton, S., & Bielick, S. (2000). *National household education survey of 1999: Data file user's manual* (Vol. I). Washington, DC: National Center for Education Statistics.

Owston, R.D. (1997). The World Wide Web: A technology to enhance teaching and learning? *Educational Researcher, 26*(2), 27-33.

Paglin, C., & Fager, J. (1997). *Alternative schools: Approaches for students at risk* (By Request series). Portland, OR: Northwest Regional Educational Laboratory: *http://www.nwrel.org/request/sept97/*

Papert, S. (1980). *Mindstorms: Children, computers, and powerful ideas.* New York: Basic Books.

Roschelle, J., & Pea, R. (1999). Trajectories from today's Web to a powerful educational structure. *Educational Researcher, 28*(5), 22-25.

Saba, F. (1999, July). Software systems in distance teaching and learning. *Distance Education Report 1999, 3*(7), 1-2. (ERIC Document Reproduction Service No. EJ591585). Retrieved May 30, 2004, from http://www.distance-educator.com/der/software.html

Sherry, L., & Hoffman, D. (1997). Web-based instruction: Barriers and facilitators. Retrieved June 7, 2004, from http://carbon.cudenver.edu/~lsherry/pubs/barriers.html

Sullivan, D. (2003). *Search engine sizes.* Retrieved May 16, 2004, from http://searchenginewatch.com/reports/article.php/2156481

U.S. Census Bureau. (2000). Current population survey design and methodology (Technical Paper 63). Washington, DC: Author.

Wallace, R. (1999). *Teaching with the Web: Challenges in a complex information space.* Retrieved June 8, 2004, from http://www.msu.edu/~ravenmw/pubs/Wallaceproposal.pdf

Wertsch, J. V. (2002). Computer mediation, PBL, and dialogicality. *Distance Education, 23*(1), 105-108.

Index

T - #0557 - 101024 - C0 - 212/152/10 - PB - 9780789024930 - Gloss Lamination